Standards-Based

SOCIAL STUDIES

Graphic Organizers & Rubrics
for Elementary Students

By Imogene Forte
and Sandra Schurr

Incentive Publications, Inc.
Nashville, Tennessee

Graphics by Joe Shibley and Jennifer J. Streams
Cover by Marta Drayton
Edited by Charlotte Bosarge

ISBN 0-86530-630-3

1   2   3   4   5   6   7   8   9   10   07   06   05   04

PRINTED IN THE UNITED STATES OF AMERICA
www.incentivepublications.com

Table of Contents

SECTION 1:
Directions for Using Graphic Organizers . . . 9

SECTION 2:
Graphic Organizers & Rubrics . . . 28

Appendix . . . 101

Index . . . 127

PREFACE

Recent research studies have confirmed a belief that intuitive teachers have long held germane to classroom success: when students are meaningfully involved in active learning tasks and in the planning and evaluation of their work, they are more enthusiastic about instructional activities, they learn and retain more, and their overall rate of achievement is greater. With the emphasis placed on measurable achievement as an overriding goal driving school system mandates, curriculum, classroom organization, and management (and even instructional practices and procedures), teachers are faced with great challenges. While striving to fulfill societal demands, they must also create and use new instructional strategies, procedures, and teaching methods to meet the diverse needs of students with widely varying backgrounds, interests, and abilities. In the rapidly changing world in which we live, and the growing avalanche of information, elementary social studies teachers are turning to student-centered instruction, active learning strategies, and authentic instruction to capture and hold students' interests and attention, and, consequently, result in increased achievement levels.

GRAPHIC ORGANIZERS

As the body of material to be covered in a given time frame grows more massive and multifaceted, and as content demands on students and teachers multiply, graphic organizers are becoming an important component of elementary social studies programs.

In the information-saturated classroom of today, sorting and making meaningful use of specific facts and concepts is becoming an increasingly important skill. Knowing where to go to find information and how to organize it once it is located is the key to processing and making meaningful use of the information gathered. Graphic organizers can be used to provide visual organization, develop scope and sequence, furnish a plan of action, aid in assessment, clarify points of interest, and/or document a process or a series of events.

The construction and use of graphic organizers encourages visual discrimination and organization, use of critical thinking skills, and meta-cognitive reflection. They can be particularly useful in helping elementary students grasp concepts and skills related to the ten standards established by the National Council for Social Studies.

In other instances, a graphic organizer may be developed as a reporting or review exercise or sometimes as a means of self-assessment after knowledge has been acquired. Graphic organizers can become valuable and effective instructional tools. The degree of their effectiveness for both students and teachers is determined by visual clarification of purpose, careful planning, organization, and attention to detail.

RUBRICS

Authentic assessment, as opposed to more traditional forms of assessment, gives both student and teacher a more realistic picture of gains made, facts learned, and information processed for retention. With rubrics, more emphasis is placed on the processing of concepts and information than on the simple recall of information. Collecting evidence from authentic assessment exercises, and taking place in realistic settings over a period of time, provides students and teachers with the most effective documentation of both skills and content mastery. Traditional measurements of student achievement such as written tests and quizzes, objective end-of-chapter tests, and standardized tests play a major role in the assessment picture as well.

The use of standards-based rubrics in elementary grade social studies classes has proven to be an extremely useful means of authentic assessment for helping students maintain interest and evaluate their own progress.

Rubrics are checklists that contain sets of criteria for measuring the elements of a product, performance, or portfolio. They can be designed as a qualitative measure (holistic rubric) to gauge overall performance of a prompt, or they can be designed as a quantitative measure (analytic rubric) to award points for each of several elements in response to a prompt.

Additional benefits from rubrics are that they require collaboration between students and teachers, are flexible and allow for individual creativity, make room for individual strengths and weaknesses, minimize competition, are meaningful to parents, allow for flexible time frames, provide multifaceted scoring systems with a variety of formats, can be sources for lively peer discussions and interaction, can include meta-cognitive reflection provisions which encourage self-awareness and critical thinking, and can help teachers determine final grades that are understood by (and hold meaning for) students.

NATIONAL STANDARDS

These standards-based graphic organizers and rubrics have been designed to provide busy elementary social studies teachers with a bank of resources from which to draw as the need arises. The ten standards developed by the National Council for Social Studies have been incorporated throughout all activities. For ease in planning, the Planning Matrix on pages 112-114 provides a complete correlation of activities to these standards.

Section 1:
Directions for Using
Graphic Organizers

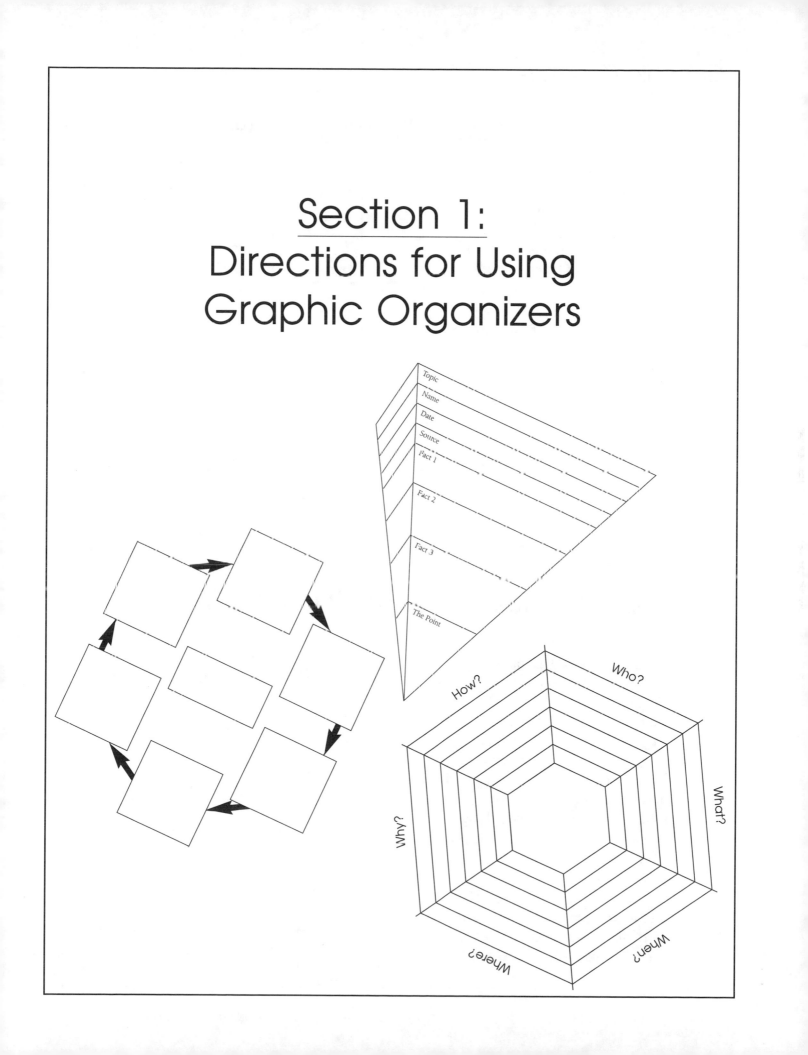

A+ Project Planning Guide

When carefully developed, this A+ Project Planning Guide will provide a blueprint for completion of a high quality project in a timely manner. It may be adapted effectively for planning and completion of a demonstration, essay, report, research paper, speech, or portfolio entry.

A reproducible copy may be found on page 29. Correlated rubric for assessment purposes may be found on page 30.

Type of Project: _____

Title and Brief Description of Project: _____

_____

_____

_____

Beginning Project Date: _____

Ending Project Date: _____

Materials Needed: _____

_____

Major Objective: _____

_____

_____

Plan of Action: _____

_____

_____

_____

Possible Problems to Overcome: _____

_____

_____

_____

Anticipated Grade from Rating Scale: _____

Actual Grade from Rating Scale: _____

Bloom's Taxonomy Book Report Outline

This Book Report Outline is based on Bloom's Taxonomy. This taxonomy developed by Benjamin Bloom provides a way to organize thinking skills into six levels from the first (most basic) level to the sixth (most complex) level. The levels are knowledge level, comprehension level, application level, analysis level, synthesis level, and, finally, evaluation level. Use of this model results in two things: application of higher-level thinking skills, and stronger reinforcement for long-lasting learning.

A reproducible copy may be found on page 31. Correlated rubric for assessment purposes may be found on page 32.

Title: _____

Author: _____

Publisher: _____ Date: _____

Evaluation

Synthesis

Analysis

Application

Comprehension

Knowledge

Graphic Organizer

Bloom's Taxonomy Plan for Studying Branches of U.S. Government

Bloom's Taxonomy Plan for Studying Branches of U.S. Government provides a way to organize thinking skills into six levels, from the first (most basic) level to the final (most complex) level of thinking.

A reproducible copy may be found on page 33.
Correlated rubric for assessment purposes may be found on page 34.

Application
Tell how the 3 branches of government related to the Constitution of the U.S. and what that means to you.

Analysis
Outline the pros and cons for a debate on giving more power to elected officials.

Comprehension
Define each of the 3 branches of the U.S. Government.

Synthesis
Pretend you are a member of the Supreme Court and you must make an important decision on making the Pledge of Allegiance a part of the school day.

Knowledge
List the 3 branches of the U.S. Government

Evaluation
Outline a speech you would make in defense of a democratic government.

Graphic Organizer

Brochure Building

Using the Brochure Building form to outline knowledge is a good way to explore, convey, and clarify social studies concepts and ideas. Students should be given a duplicated copy of the graphic organizer itself, instructed to fold the indicated sections on the dotted lines, and then told to complete each of the six sections (three per side) following the guidelines for recording and discussing their ideas. Finally, each section should be labeled 1 through 6.

Section 1: Write student name, date, and the social studies-related topic for this brochure.

Section 2: Write down a series of important facts or key things to remember about this topic.

Section 3: Write down some specific and concrete examples of this topic in action to show how it works.

Section 4: Write out some questions one might ask of others to test what they know about this topic.

Section 5: Write down the correct answers to these questions that a person would accept as valid.

Section 6: Construct a drawing or model of something related to this topic.

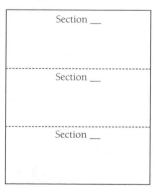

A reproducible copy may be found on page 35.
Correlated rubric for assessment purposes may be found on page 36.

Standards-Based SOCIAL STUDIES
Graphic Organizers & Rubrics for Elementary Students

Calendar Organizer

The Calendar Organizer is a valuable organizational tool for use in all content areas. A blank calendar may be used to create a portfolio artifact, to serve as the basis of an outline or a time line for a project or course of study, as a record-keeping device for homework or classroom assignments, as a peer tutoring or cooperative learning aid, or as a teacher-directed instructional tool.

A reproducible copy may be found on page 37. Correlated rubric for assessment purposes may be found on page 38.

Friday				
Thursday				
Wednesday				
Tuesday				
Monday				
	Knowledge/ Comprehension	Comprehension/ Application/ Analysis	Analysis/ Synthesis	Evaluation

Cultural Influences Chart

The Cultural Influences Chart may be useful in identifying persons of significant importance to a specific culture in a particular period of history. The major players or characters that were important to the activities and outcomes in significant ways are identified, and their contributions (both positive and negative) are analyzed.

This tool may be equally useful for studying a country or a region with the headings changed to reflect appropriate topics (example: geography, economics, government, etc.) rather than specific persons or cultures.

A reproducible copy may be found on page 39. Correlated rubric for assessment purposes may be found on page 40.

Heroes	Decision-Makers	Challenges
Facilitators	Conformists	Outcomes

Graphic Organizer

Cycle Graph

The Cycle Graph can be used to identify events that tend to be circular or cyclical in nature. The title of the topic or event should be recorded in the rectangular box. Then, the events or situations that must take place are listed in a clockwise fashion. Additional boxes may be inserted anywhere in the cycle as needed.

A reproducible copy may be found on page 41. Correlated rubric for assessment purposes may be found on page 42.

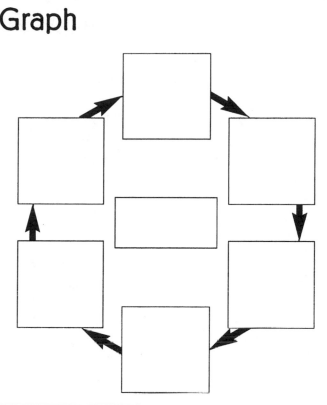

Graphic Organizer

Family Tree Organizer

The Family Tree Organizer provides an organizational structure for collecting and organizing information about the heritage and individual members of a particular family. The top box is used for the family name, place or origin, important dates, and other unique facts. The other boxes can then be used to record individual family heads and offspring (with supporting dates). This tool may be used to help students trace their own heritage, or as an aid for studying the life of a historically significant person.

A reproducible copy may be found on page 43. Correlated rubric for assessment purposes may be found on page 44.

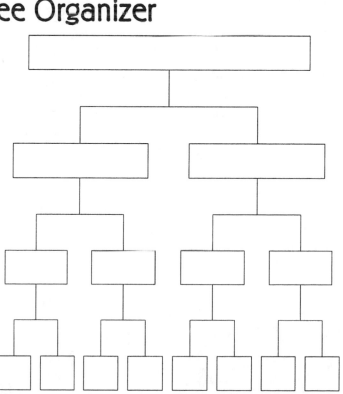

Standards-Based SOCIAL STUDIES
Graphic Organizers & Rubrics for Elementary Students

Graphic Organizer

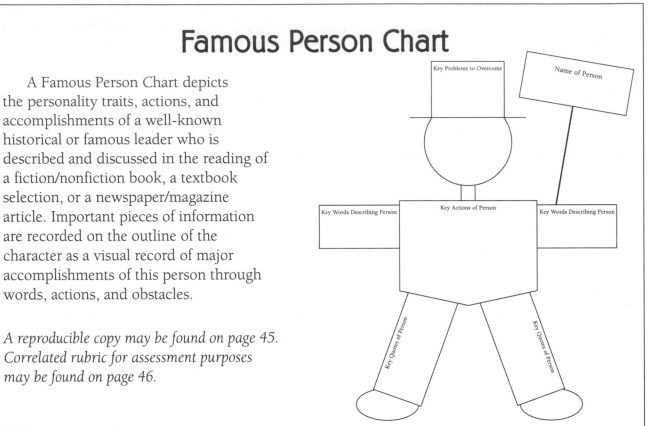

Famous Person Chart

A Famous Person Chart depicts the personality traits, actions, and accomplishments of a well-known historical or famous leader who is described and discussed in the reading of a fiction/nonfiction book, a textbook selection, or a newspaper/magazine article. Important pieces of information are recorded on the outline of the character as a visual record of major accomplishments of this person through words, actions, and obstacles.

A reproducible copy may be found on page 45. Correlated rubric for assessment purposes may be found on page 46.

Key Problems to Overcome

Name of Person

Key Words Describing Person

Key Actions of Person

Key Words Describing Person

Key Quotes of Person

Key Quotes of Person

Graphic Organizer

Filmstrip Organizer

Students should use the various sections of the Filmstrip Organizer to draw and describe how social studies concepts relate to other subject areas in school or how they relate to their everyday lives. Students should draw a different picture or diagram in each frame, then write a simple sentence under each frame that states the real-world application or connection. This organizer may be duplicated several times to add extra frames as needed for reporting of information.

A reproducible copy may be found on page 47. Correlated rubric for assessment purposes may be found on page 48.

Standards-Based SOCIAL STUDIES
Graphic Organizers & Rubrics for Elementary Students

Copyright ©2004 by Incentive Publications, Inc.
Nashville, TN.

Graphic Organizer

5 Ws and How Web

The 5 Ws and How Web may be used to record the who, when, where, why, and how of a magazine article, a newspaper article, or an excerpt from a classroom textbook. The article or chapter titles are written in the center hexagon and the answers to questions about the situation are written in the appropriate web sections. A paragraph is then created to summarize the information from this web.

A reproducible copy may be found on page 49. Correlated rubric for assessment purposes may be found on page 50.

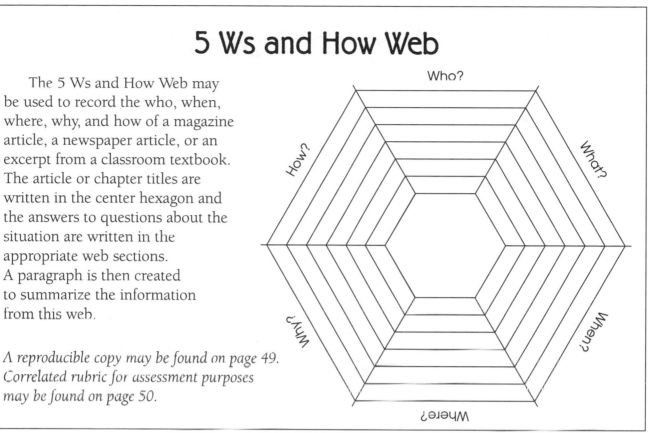

Graphic Organizer

Flowchart Organizer

Flowchart Organizers are used to organize a sequence of events, actions, or decisions.

A standard set of symbols is used when designing flowcharts so that everyone can understand and use the same symbols. The arrangement of the symbols will vary according to the type of sequence depicted.

The example explains the symbols and how each one is used. Flowcharts will need to be created on unlined, blank paper to suit individual situations.

A reproducible copy may be found on page 51. Correlated rubric for assessment purposes may be found on page 52.

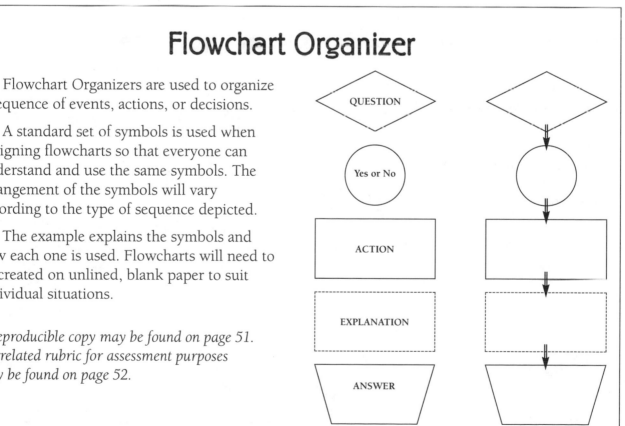

Get the Point Organizer

The Get the Point Organizer is especially valuable in helping students gather and synthesize information related to a specific topic. As facts are recorded and consequently reviewed with the goal of reaching a logical conclusion, active learning takes place in a personal manner providing for higher-level thinking and retention of facts and impressions.

A reproducible copy may be found on page 53. Correlated rubric for assessment purposes may be found on page 54.

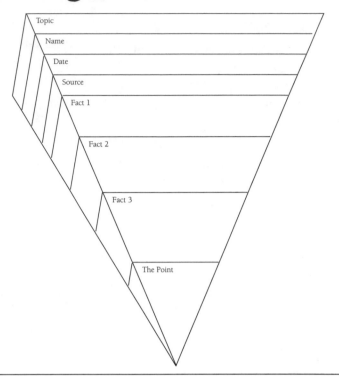

Topic

Name

Date

Source

Fact 1

Fact 2

Fact 3

The Point

Graphic Organizer

Group Project Plan Organizer

A Group Project Plan Organizer will facilitate group collaboration and planning. When thoughtfully completed, it will provide an easy-to-read-and-follow visual plan to show who is to do what, when, how, where, and with what.

A reproducible copy may be found on page 55.
Correlated rubric for assessment purposes may be found on page 56.

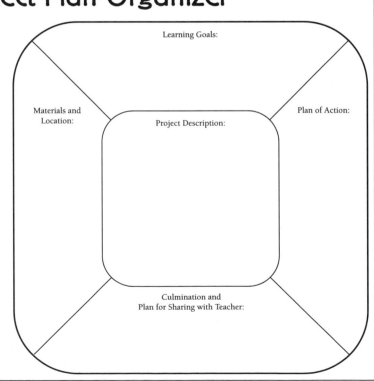

Learning Goals:

Materials and Location:

Project Description:

Plan of Action:

Culmination and Plan for Sharing with Teacher:

Group Rating Scale

The Group Rating Scale can be especially valuable when used as a cooperative learning tool. It helps to improve individual as well as group contributions to the achievement of a mutually determined goal. When used at the beginning of group work (and again at the conclusion) it can provide insight on the success of failure of the group's teamwork, efficient, and effectiveness.

A reproducible copy may be found on page 57. Correlated rubric for assessment purposes may be found on page 58.

	Excellent	Good	Fair	Poor
Group Interaction				
Individual Contributions				
Role Assignments				
Objectives				
Plan of Action				
Materials				
Use of Time				
Overall Rating				

Independent Study Planning Tool

The Independent Study Planning Tool form may be used to map out a game plan for completing an independent study of a specific topic, an author's work, or a current event of particular significance. Since this planning tool is flexible in nature to allow for individual creativity, it is important that details and plans for completing the study are recorded accurately and are very specific in nature.

A reproducible copy may be found on page 59. Correlated rubric for assessment purposes may be found on page 60.

PERSONAL PROJECT PLAN

Title and Description of Study	Beginning Date	Format for Study
	_____	
	Completion Date	
	_____	

Resources Needed and Location

Challenges to be expected and/or questions to answer

Method of Evaluation

Interview Organizer

The Interview Organizer is designed to structure an interview that a student might conduct with another person of interest. It requires an advanced set of questions as well as spaces for recording the interviewee's responses. The most important item on the interview organizer is "purpose of the interview." The interviewee should use the rest of the items on the sheet to clarify and reinforce the reason for this interview, and, consequently, how the information will be used.

A reproducible copy may be found on page 61. Correlated rubric for assessment purposes may be found on page 62.

Getting Ready for the Interview
Name of Interviewee _____
Name of Interviewer _____
Date of Interview _____
Purpose of Interview _____
_____

Conducting the Interview
Question One _____
_____
Response _____
_____
Question Two _____
_____
Response _____
_____
Question Three _____
_____
Response _____

Following the Interview
Results of the Interview _____
_____
_____
_____

KWL Organizer

A KWL Organizer guides students through a three-step process by recording a series of knowledge-based statements, a set of questions, and items learned as part of a research or reading task. Before investigating a topic, students should write down facts they know in the K column (or *What I Know* column), questions they hope to find answers to in the W column (or *What I Want to Know* column), and information learned in the L column (or *What I Learned* column).

A reproducible copy may be found on page 63. Correlated rubric for assessment purposes may be found on page 64.

Topic of Study/Title _____
Student's Name _____

What I Know	What I Want to Know	What I Learned

Main Idea Map

A Main Idea Map is built around a main idea (or central concept) important to the study of a given topic. Other thoughts related to the main idea in some meaningful way are recorded as extensions or associations of the main concept through a series of adjacent lines and circles. This organizational tool will help students to develop and use comprehension, application, and analysis skills in order to evaluate and synthesize scattered ideas related to a specific topic. It may also be used as an effective guide for teacher-directed study aimed at reinforcement extension of previously learned concepts.

A reproducible copy may be found on page 65. Correlated rubric for assessment purposes may be found on page 66.

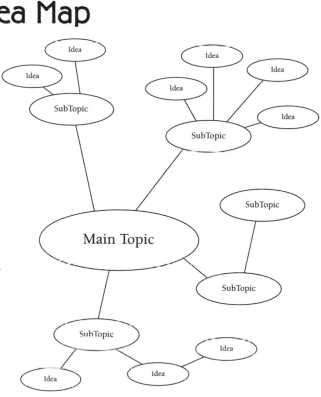

Observation Log

An Observation Log is a collection of simple but informative entries about a given topic or subject. Observation logs are used to watch something closely over a period of time and to record the changes observed during this process. All entries require a date and time for the observation as well as a few lines describing what is seen.

A reproducible copy may be found on page 67. Correlated rubric for assessment purposes may be found on page 68.

Date: _____ Time: _____
Observation: _____

Date: _____ Time: _____
Observation: _____

Planning Tree Organizer

Use the Planning Tree Organizer for organizing and completing a project that has a major goal and sub-goals to accomplish through a variety of sequential tasks. The major goal is written in the large circle while sub-goals are written in the medium-sized circles. Finally, the sequence or facts of tasks for the implementation of the goals is organized on the lines below the small circles. It is important that each set of tasks be grouped with the appropriate sub-goal in the diagram.

A reproducible copy may be found on page 69. Correlated rubric for assessment purposes may be found on page 70.

Pro or Con Chart

The Pro or Con Chart is a tool for recording the arguments for and against a given position when studying a controversial problem, issue, or decision.

In the umbrella, the student is to write the main topic or issue to be considered. In the left-hand column, the student is to write the "pros" or "reasons for" the topic or issue, in the right-hand column, the student is to write the "cons" or "reasons against" the topic or issue.

A reproducible copy may be found on page 71. Correlated rubric for assessment purposes may be found on page 72.

Topic/Issue

Pros   Cons

Problem-Solving Star

The Problem-Solving Star encourages consideration of various solutions to a specific problem. The problem is written in the center of the star and the key points to consider (or potential solutions to the problem) are written on the five points of the star. Space on back of the star can then be used to state the best possible solution to the problem once each point has been weighed and objectively considered.

A reproducible copy may be found on page 73. Correlated rubric for assessment purposes may be found on page 74.

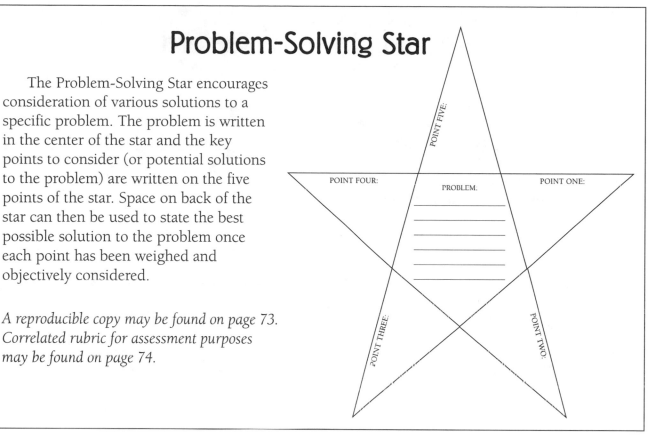

Puzzle Pieces Organizer

The Puzzle Pieces Organizer allows students to research a topic and record separate facts or pieces of information gleaned from the readings on individual puzzle pieces. These puzzle pieces can then be reviewed or the information recorded can be organized and rewritten meaningfully to produce a short report summary.

A reproducible copy may be found on page 75. Correlated rubric for assessment purposes may be found on page 76.

Reading to Learn Record

The Reading to Learn Record may be used to sort out and record information from various sections of a social studies textbook or other reference book. Select a chapter in the text, then write down information you would like to know from each section of the chapter (before you read it) and then what you learned from the chapter (after you read it).

A reproducible copy may be found on page 77. Correlated rubric for assessment purposes may be found on page 78.

	Section Title	What I Expect to Learn	What I Learned
1.			
2.			
3.			
4.			
5.			
6.			
7.			
8.			
9.			
10.			

Graphic Organizer

Scope and Sequence Ladder

The Scope and Sequence Ladder can be used for creating a time line, organizing a historical sequence of events, or outlining a series of tasks to perform. On the first rung of the ladder, write the first date, event, or step of your task. On the second rung of the ladder, write the second date, event or step of your task. Continue in this way with the third, fourth, and fifth rungs. You may use additional ladders if you have a need for more "rungs" in your planning.

A reproducible copy may be found on page 79. Correlated rubric for assessment purposes may be found on page 80.

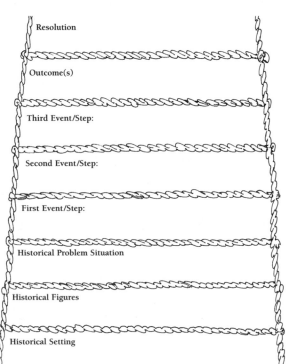

Resolution

Outcome(s)

Third Event/Step:

Second Event/Step:

First Event/Step:

Historical Problem Situation

Historical Figures

Historical Setting

Graphic Organizer

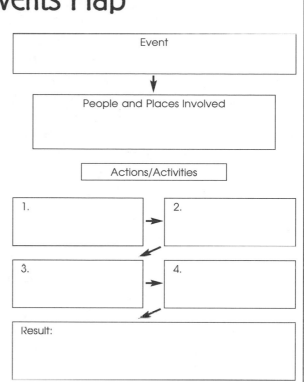

Sequence of Events Map

The Sequence of Events Map will enable students to choose a historical or economic-related event and record the key pieces of information in the appropriate places in order to keep track of the most significant people, places, and actions associated with the event. It can be especially useful for a small group, for peer tutoring, or for gathering information for a report. It can also serve as an organizational tool for total-class teacher-guided study.

A reproducible copy may be found on page 81. Correlated rubric for assessment purposes may be found on page 82.

Graphic Organizer

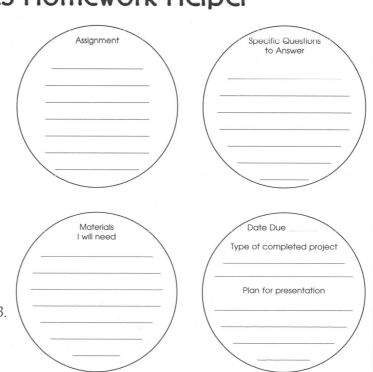

Social Studies Homework Helper

The Social Studies Homework Helper will serve as a planning tool to help a student plan for completion of homework assignments in a timely fashion. The simplicity of the organizer, coupled with very specific objectives and time factors, will serve to keep the student focused on the major objectives while at the same time providing very specific objectives and time limitations.

A reproducible copy may be found on page 83. Correlated rubric for assessment purposes may be found on page 84.

Storyboard Organizer

A Storyboard Organizer is used to describe a series of events in chronological order. Pieces of information, ideas, thoughts, or situations (based on when and how they occurred) may be assembled easily for review and reflection. This organizer is especially valuable in helping to identify events leading up to a conflict, war, election, historical moment, discovery, invention, disaster, or exploration.

A reproducible copy may be found on page 85. Correlated rubric for assessment purposes may be found on page 86.

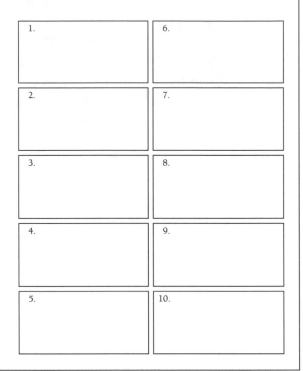

Study Guide for Preparing a Social Studies Project

This Study Guide for Preparing a Social Studies Project easily helps students to assimilate the information taught from their reading and from their classwork. It will assist them in separating the information required to complete a structured social studies project.

A reproducible copy may be found on page 87. Correlated rubric for assessment purposes may be found on page 88.

Study Guide for Preparing for a Social Studies Quiz

This organizer will be helpful to a student when collecting, analyzing, studying, and reviewing notes during preparation for a test. Not only will it help in gathering the main ideas, topics, and facts needed for the quiz, but it also will teach the student to formulate and maintain an organized study plan.

A reproducible copy may be found on page 89. Correlated rubric for assessment purposes may be found on page 90.

1. Major Topics to be covered on the test	2. Sub-Topics

3. Materials to be reviewed (textbooks, class notes, handouts, my own work)	4. Facts to Review

My Study Plan:

1.
2.
3.
4.
5.
6
7.
8.

Surfing the Net Organizer

The Surfing the Net Organizer is designed to aid students in locating and using a variety of websites to obtain and organize information related to different genres of literature. As the website for each genre is located, it is recorded in the specified circle. Each website should be accompanied by descriptive sentences or key words or phrases.

A reproducible copy may be found on page 91. Correlated rubric for assessment purposes may be found on page 92.

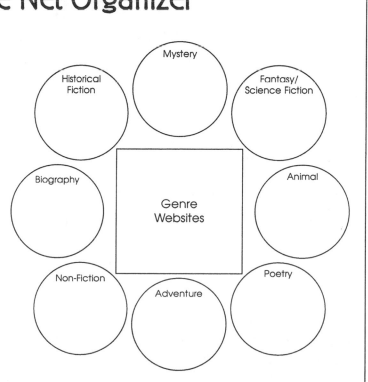

Standards-Based SOCIAL STUDIES
Graphic Organizers & Rubrics for Elementary Students

Graphic Organizer

Venn Diagram

A Venn Diagram consists of several large intersecting circles that are used to compare and contrast three different (but related) objects, concepts, events, or persons. The intersecting parts of the circles are used to record common elements of the three items while the outer parts of the circles are used to record elements uniquely appropriate for any one of the items. This diagram may be especially useful for comparing/contrasting cultures, for examining physical or historical features of countries, states, or regions, or for looking at one's own background or beliefs.

A reproducible copy may be found on page 93. Correlated rubric for assessment purposes may be found on page 94.

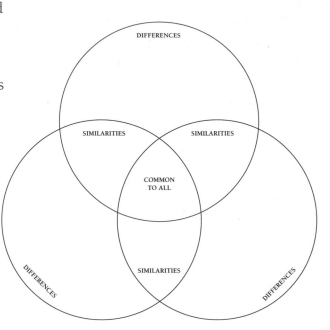

Graphic Organizer

What, So What, Now What? Chart

A What, So What, and Now What? Chart organizes thinking after reading a story, textbook section, or article on a given topic by requiring reflection back over the information presented.

The What? column requires the student to write down a response to the question: What did I learn from this selection?

The So What? column requires the student to write down a series of responses to the question: What difference does it make now that I know this?

The Now What? column asks students to write down some thoughts answering the question: How can I use this information to make a difference in what I know or can do?

A reproducible copy may be found on page 95. Correlated rubric for assessment purposes may be found on page 96.

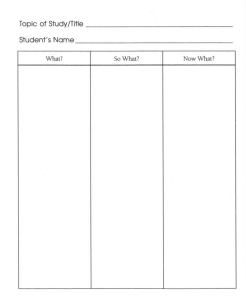

Williams' Taxonomy Lesson Plan

Using Williams' Taxonomy Lesson Plan to develop a lesson plan enables the learner to explore a social, political, or historical situation or event in a more original and creative manner in order to come up with understandings and/or conclusions of a unique nature. It can be especially valuable as a guide for long-term group work with some degree of teacher guidance, or for carefully planned independent study projects. *See page 123 in the appendix for a more thorough presentation of Williams' Taxonomy.*

A reproducible copy may be found on page 97. Correlated rubric for assessment purposes may be found on page 98.

	ACTIVITY 1	ACTIVITY 2	ACTIVITY 3
FLUENCY			
FLEXIBILITY			
ORIGINALITY			
ELABORATION			
RISK TAKING			
COMPLEXITY			
CURIOSITY			
IMAGINATION			

Word Keeper Bookmark

The Word Keeper Bookmark will aid students both in keeping track of previously unfamiliar words and in completion of social studies homework assignments. Create each bookmark by cutting on the dotted line; it may then be decorated on the back with appropriate illustrations to provide interest and motivation, or be used for additional teacher instructions or information (examples: social studies facts, research, library, or media information, etc.). One of the Word Keeper Bookmark's most attractive features is its adaptability to positioning inside a textbook or student planner. Holes can be punched for a loose-leaf notebook if desired. The format may also be adapted for word lists, unit planning, or ongoing facts or plans for a unit or project.

A reproducible copy may be found on page 99. Correlated rubric for assessment purposes may be found on page 100.

Homework for week of	Homework for week of	Homework for week of	Homework for week of
Subject	Subject	Subject	Subject
Assignment	Assignment	Assignment	Assignment
References/ Textbook pages	References/ Textbook pages	References/ Textbook pages	References/ Textbook pages
Due date	Due date	Due date	Due date
Notes	Notes	Notes	Notes
Grade/Teacher Comments	Grade/Teacher Comments	Grade/Teacher Comments	Grade/Teacher Comments
Student's Name	Student's Name	Student's Name	Student's Name

Standards-Based SOCIAL STUDIES
Graphic Organizers & Rubrics for Elementary Students

Section 2:
Graphic Organizers
& Rubrics

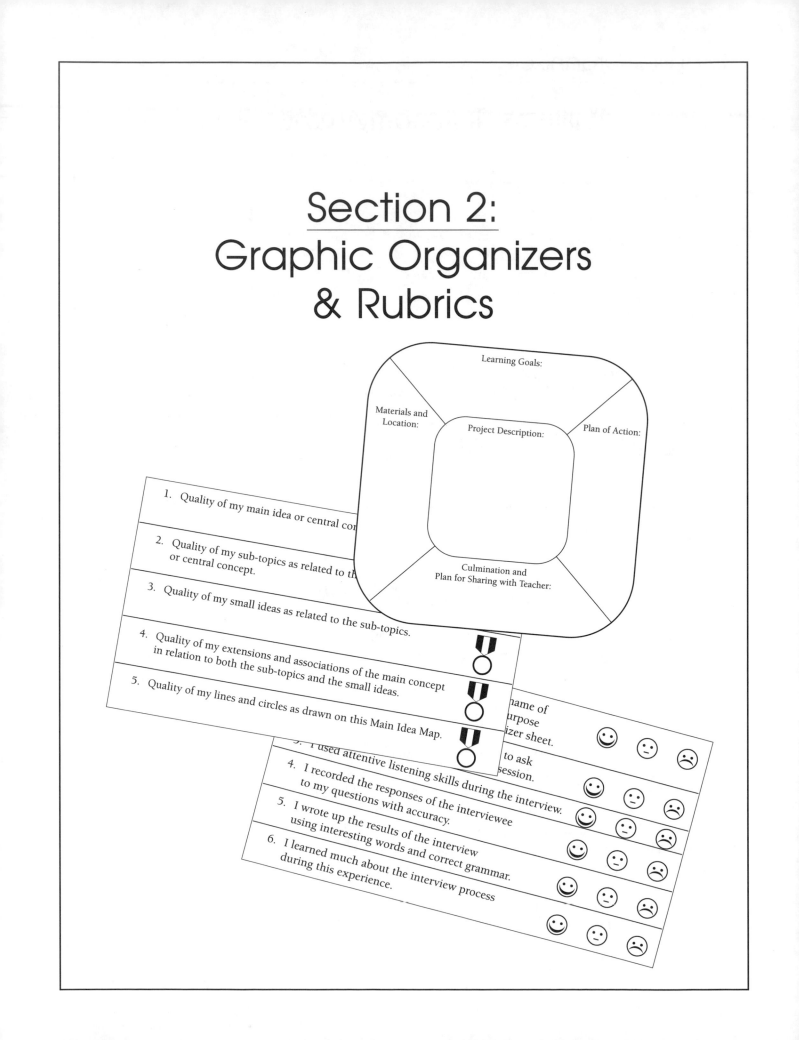

Learning Goals:

Materials and
Location:

Project Description:

Plan of Action:

Culmination and
Plan for Sharing with Teacher:

1. Quality of my main idea or central con

2. Quality of my sub-topics as related to th
   or central concept.

3. Quality of my small ideas as related to the sub-topics.

4. Quality of my extensions and associations of the main concept
   in relation to both the sub-topics and the small ideas.

5. Quality of my lines and circles as drawn on this Main Idea Map.

name of
urpose
izer sheet.

to ask
session.

3. I used attentive listening skills during the interview.

4. I recorded the responses of the interviewee
   to my questions with accuracy.

5. I wrote up the results of the interview
   using interesting words and correct grammar.

6. I learned much about the interview process
   during this experience.

A+ Project Planning Guide

Graphic Organizer

Type of Project: _____

Title and Brief Description of Project: _____

_____

_____

_____

_____

Beginning Project Date: _____

Ending Project Date: _____

Materials Needed: _____

_____

_____

Major Objective: _____

_____

_____

_____

Plan of Action: _____

_____

_____

_____

Possible Problems to Overcome: _____

_____

_____

_____

Anticipated Grade from Rating Scale:_____

Actual Grade from Rating Scale: _____

Standards-Based SOCIAL STUDIES
Graphic Organizers & Rubrics for Elementary Students

A+ Project Planning Guide

Rating Scale:

	A	B	C
	Absolute Best	Better	Could Be Better

Directions to Student:

In the box at the end of each line, write the letter that best describes your performance on this activity.

1. I chose an appropriate topic for this project.	☐
2. I gave my project a good title and wrote a brief description of the subject.	☐
3. I began and ended the project in a timely fashion.	☐
4. I located the necessary materials to complete the project.	☐
5. I wrote the major objective for the project.	☐
6. I developed a plan of action for the project.	☐
7. I anticipated possible problems to overcome before starting the project and was able to resolve them to my satisfaction.	☐
8. My anticipated grade for the project matched the actual grade I received.	☐

Comments by Student: _____

_____

_____

Signed _____ Date _____

Comments by Teacher: _____

_____

_____

Signed _____ Date _____

Bloom's Taxonomy Book Report Outline

Title: _____

Author: _____

Publisher: _____ Date: _____

Evaluation

Synthesis

Analysis

Application

Comprehension

Knowledge

Bloom's Taxonomy Book Report Outline

Rubric

Rating Scale:

 1
Full Bloom

 2
Ready to Bloom

 3
Just-Planted Seeds

Directions to Student:

In the flower at the end of each line, write the number that best describes your work.

1. My choice for the biography was appropriate for this assignment.	✿
2. My responses to the Knowledge Level questions were complete.	✿
3. My responses to the Comprehension Level questions were adequate.	✿
4. My responses to the Application tasks were well done.	✿
5. My response to the Analysis task was acceptable.	✿
6. My response to the Synthesis task was creative and interesting.	✿
7. My response to the Evaluation task was a good one.	✿

Comments by Student: _____

_____

_____

Signed _____ Date _____

Comments by Teacher: _____

_____

_____

Signed _____ Date _____

Standards-Based SOCIAL STUDIES
Graphic Organizers & Rubrics for Elementary Students

Copyright ©2004 by Incentive Publications, Inc.
Nashville, TN.

Bloom's Taxonomy Plan for Studying Branches of U.S. Government

Application
Tell how the 3 branches of government related to the Constitution of the U.S. and what that means to you.

Analysis
Outline the pros and cons for a debate on giving more power to elected officials.

Comprehension
Define each of the 3 branches of the U.S. Government.

Synthesis
Pretend you are a member of the Supreme Court and you must make an important decision on making the Pledge of Allegiance a part of the school day.

Knowledge
List the 3 branches of the U.S. Government.

Evaluation
Outline a speech you would make in defense of a democratic government.

Topic _____

Resources Needed _____

Resource Location _____

Completion Date _____

Student Signature: _____ Date: _____

Teacher Signature: _____ Date: _____

Standards-Based SOCIAL STUDIES
Graphic Organizers & Rubrics for Elementary Students

Bloom's Taxonomy Plan for Studying Branches of U.S. Government

Rubric

Rating Scale: 3   2   1
                 Strong   Fair   Needs Improvement

Directions to Student:

In the box at the top of each larger box, write the number that best describes your work using Bloom's Taxonomy. Then, briefly defend your choice with a descriptive comment.

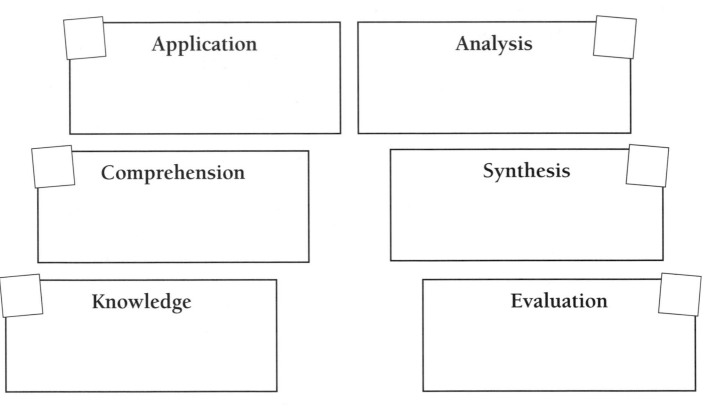

Application	Analysis
Comprehension	Synthesis
Knowledge	Evaluation

Follow Up:

Which levels of Bloom's Taxonomy were the easiest for you to do and why?

_____

_____

_____

Which levels of Bloom's Taxonomy were the most difficult for you to do and why?

_____

_____

_____

Standards-Based SOCIAL STUDIES
Graphic Organizers & Rubrics for Elementary Students

Copyright ©2004 by Incentive Publications, Inc.
Nashville, TN.

Brochure Building

Section ___

Section ___

Section ___

Brochure Building

Rating Scale:

H	S	L
High Degree	Satisfactory Degree	Limited Degree

Directions to Student:

In the box at the end of each line, write the letter that describes your work.

1. I chose an appropriate social studies topic for my brochure.	☐
2. I did adequate research on my social studies topic.	☐
3. I understood my social studies topic well.	☐
4. I wrote down several important social studies-related facts and key things to remember in my brochure.	☐
5. I gave specific and concrete social studies examples in this topic to show how things work out.	☐
6. I included some good questions with their answers on this topic for others to read about.	☐
7. I constructed a quality drawing or model of something related to this social studies topic.	☐

Directions to Student:

In the space below, draw a sketch of your brochure cover complete with title.

Calendar Organizer

Graphic Organizer

	Monday	Tuesday	Wednesday	Thursday	Friday
Knowledge/ Comprehension					
Comprehension/ Application/ Analysis					
Analysis/ Synthesis					
Evaluation					

Standards-Based SOCIAL STUDIES
Graphic Organizers & Rubrics for Elementary Students

Calendar Organizer

Rating Scale:

1	2	3
No Progress	Some Progress	Great Progress

Directions to Student:

In the box at the end of each line, write the number that best describes your performance on this activity.

1. I understand the multiple purposes of this calendar organizer.	☐
2. I have used this calendar organizer successfully.	☐
3. I find this calendar organizer helps me as a learning tool.	☐
4. I check and/or proof my entries on this calendar organizer whenever necessary.	☐
5. I feel this calendar organizer has improved my overall organizational skills.	☐

My primary use of this organizational calendar has been _____

_____

_____

I might try using this organizational calendar next time to _____

_____

_____

The most difficult part of completing this organizational calendar for me seems to be _____

_____

Questions or remarks for my student/teacher conference: _____

_____

_____

Cultural Influences Chart

Location _____ Date _____

Heroes	Decision-Makers	Challenges
Facilitators	Conformists	Outcomes

Standards-Based SOCIAL STUDIES
Graphic Organizers & Rubrics for Elementary Students

Cultural Influences Chart

Rating Scale:

3	2	1
Outstanding	Satisfactory	Needs Improvement

Directions to Student:

In the box at the end of each line, write the number that best describes your work on this activity.

1. I have chosen a manageable culture to study for this project. ☐

2. I have a working definition of each of these words: ☐
   - Heroes
   - Victims
   - Facilitators
   - Troublemakers
   - Decision-Makers
   - Leaders
   - Conformists
   - Pacifists

3. I have been able to identify the major players or characters that were important to the development of this culture. ☐
   - Heroes
   - Victims
   - Facilitators
   - Troublemakers
   - Decision-Makers
   - Leaders
   - Conformists
   - Pacifists

4. I have researched information on each of these major players or characters and can share details about them in interesting ways. ☐
   - Heroes
   - Victims
   - Facilitators
   - Troublemakers
   - Decision-Makers
   - Leaders
   - Conformists
   - Pacifists

Comments by Student: _____

_____

_____

_____

Signed _____ Date _____

Comments by Teacher: _____

_____

_____

Signed _____ Date _____

Cycle Graph

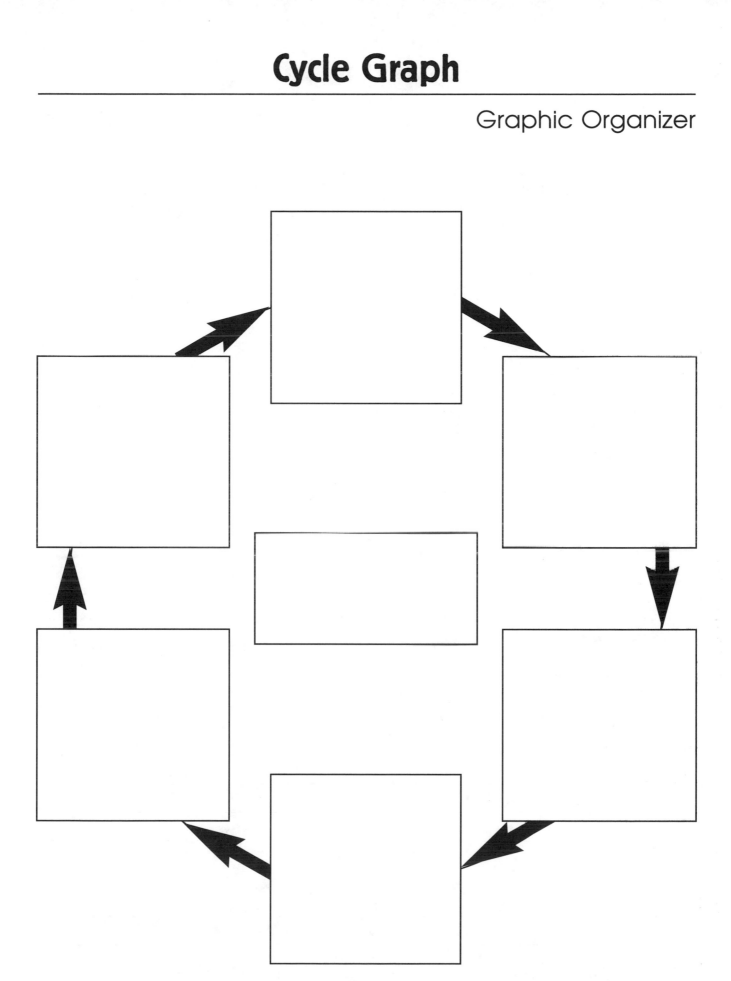

Standards-Based SOCIAL STUDIES
Graphic Organizers & Rubrics for Elementary Students

Cycle Graph

Rubric

Rating Scale:

● Very Well   ◐ Somewhat   ○ Not At All

Directions to Student:

Fill in the circle at the end of each line to the level that matches your work on this activity.

1. I understand the purpose of the Cycle Graph.	⊖
2. I understand the concepts of "circular" and "cyclical" when applied to social studies topics or themes.	⊖
3. I am able to record events or situations in the boxes on the Cycle Graph in their correct sequence.	⊖
4. I am able to insert additional boxes on the Cycle Graph as needed.	⊖
5. I am able interpret and explain my completed Cycle Graph to others.	⊖
6. I would know when to use the Cycle Graph as an organizational structure in future situations.	⊖

Comments by Student: _____

_____

_____

Signed _____ Date _____

Comments by Teacher: _____

_____

_____

Signed _____ Date _____

Family Tree Organizer

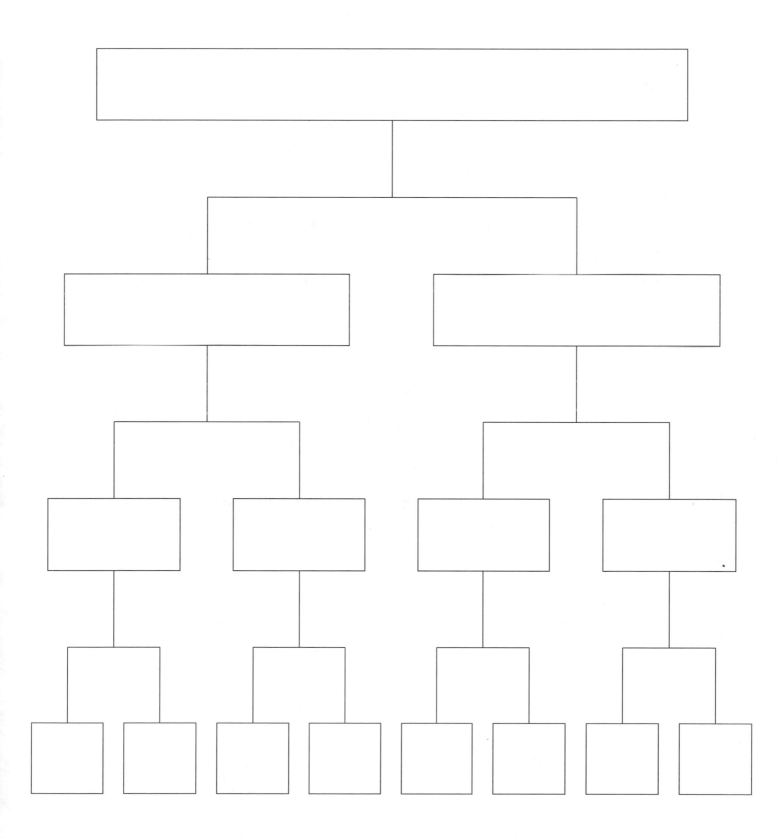

Standards-Based SOCIAL STUDIES
Graphic Organizers & Rubrics for Elementary Students

Family Tree Organizer

Rating Scale:

      3 = Excellent   2 = Fair   1 = Poor

Directions to Student:

In the box at the end of each line, write the number describes your work.

1. I learned a lot about the function of a Family Tree.	☐
2. I learned a lot about my family heritage from this assignment.	☐
3. I learned a lot of new names of members in my family.	☐
4. I learned a lot of dates important to my family.	☐
5. I learned a lot of unique facts about my family and its members.	☐
6. I learned a lot about offspring of family heads related to me.	☐

Here are some hypothetical names of family members and their offspring that I would like to see added to my family tree in the future.

Name   Relationship to Me

_____   _____

_____   _____

_____   _____

_____   _____

_____   _____

_____   _____

Famous Person Chart

Graphic Organizer

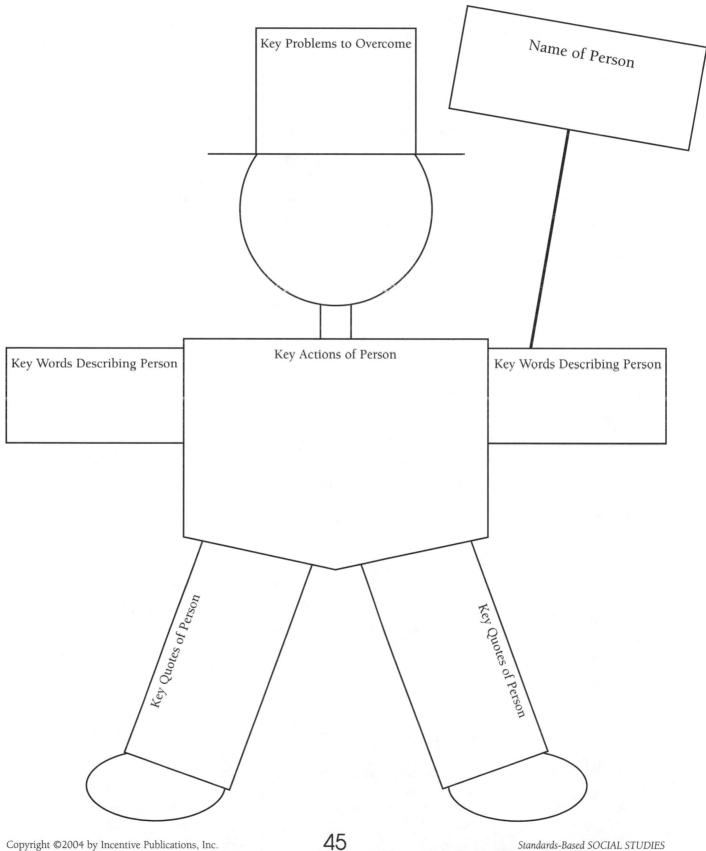

Name of Person

Key Problems to Overcome

Key Words Describing Person

Key Actions of Person

Key Words Describing Person

Key Quotes of Person

Key Quotes of Person

Standards-Based SOCIAL STUDIES
Graphic Organizers & Rubrics for Elementary Students

Famous Person Chart

Rating Scale:

√–	√	√+
Needs more work	OK	Great Work

Directions to Student/Teacher:

Place the appropriate mark in the box at the end of each question.

	Student	Teacher
1. Quality of Work: Selection Process for Famous Person		
2. Quality of Work: Key Problems Famous Person Had to Overcome		
3. Quality of Work: Key Words Describing Person		
4. Quality of Work: Key Actions of Person		
5. Quality of Work: Key Quotes of Person		
6. Quality of Work: Research on Problems, Words, Actions, and Deeds of Person		

The strongest feature of this Famous Person Chart is:

Student _____

Teacher _____

The weakest feature of this Famous Person Chart is:

Student _____

Teacher _____

Recommendation for improvement:

Student _____

Teacher _____

Filmstrip Organizer

Standards-Based SOCIAL STUDIES
Graphic Organizers & Rubrics for Elementary Students

Filmstrip Organizer

Rating Scale:

Wonderful
● ● ●

Pretty Good Job
○ ● ●

Not Good
○ ○ ○

Directions to Student:

Color in the correct number of circles that best describes your work for each item listed below.

1. I have chosen a great topic for my filmstrip project.	○ ○ ○
2. I have been able to relate a social studies concept to my everyday life as part of this project.	○ ○ ○
3. I have completed enough frames to adequately describe and explain the ideas in my project.	○ ○ ○
4. I have drawn a different picture or diagram in each frame of this project.	○ ○ ○
5. I have written a simple but informative sentence under each frame that shows the real-world application or connection as part of this project.	○ ○ ○
6. I have added extra frames as needed to complete my project.	○ ○ ○
7. I am very proud of this project.	○ ○ ○

Comments by Student: _____

_____

_____

Signed _____ Date _____

Comments by Teacher: _____

_____

_____

Signed _____ Date _____

5 Ws and How Web

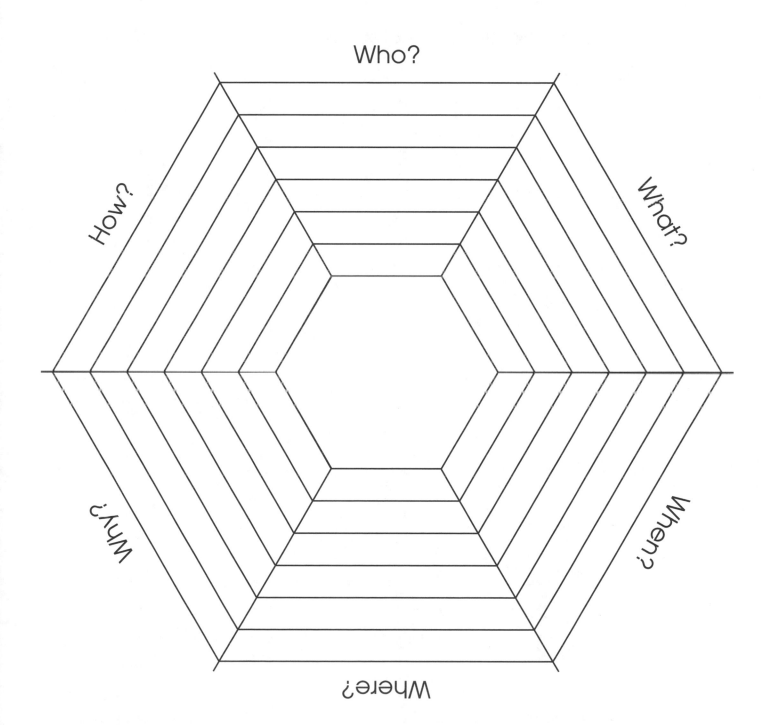

Who?

What?

When?

Where?

Why?

How?

5Ws and How Web

Rating Scale:

Star Reporter	Desk Reporter	Cub Reporter
★ ★ ★	★ ★ ☆	☆ ☆ ☆

Directions to Student:

In the box at the end of each line, shade in the appropriate number of stars for your performance on this activity.

1. My "WHO" response is complete.	☆ ☆ ☆
2. My "WHAT" response is complete.	☆ ☆ ☆
3. My "WHEN" response is complete.	☆ ☆ ☆
4. My "WHERE" response is complete.	☆ ☆ ☆
5. My "WHY" response is complete.	☆ ☆ ☆
6. My "HOW" response is complete.	☆ ☆ ☆
7. My "SUMMARY" response is complete.	☆ ☆ ☆

Comments by Student: _____

_____

_____

Signed _____ Date _____

Comments by Teacher: _____

_____

_____

Signed _____ Date _____

Flowchart Organizer

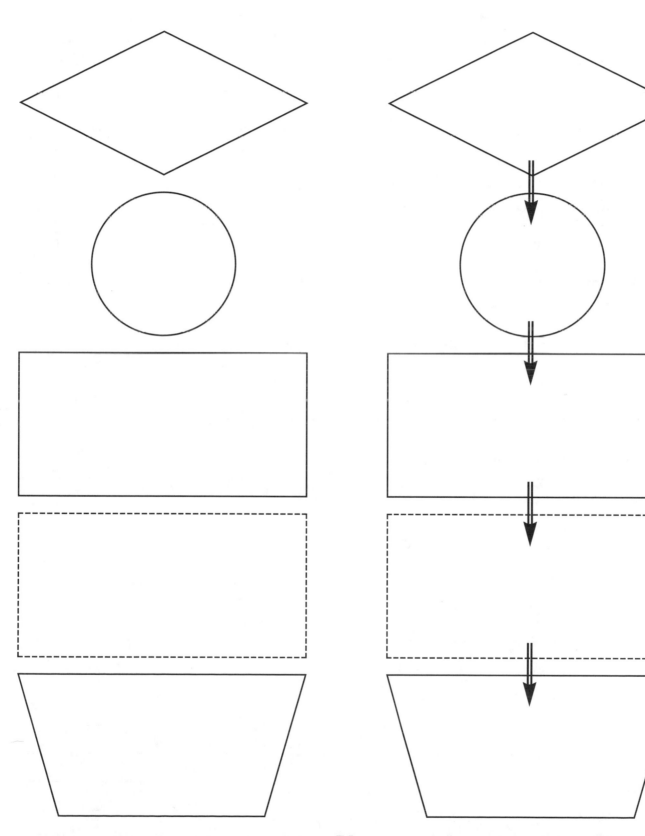

Standards-Based SOCIAL STUDIES
Graphic Organizers & Rubrics for Elementary Students

Flowchart Organizer

Rating Scale:

3	2	1
Terrific Flow	Good Flow	Poor Flow

Directions to Student:

In the box at the end of each line, write the number that best describes your work.

1. I learned how to construct a flowchart that organizes sequences of events, actions, or decisions.	☐
2. I learned how to interpret the symbols for constructing flowcharts.	☐
3. I learned how to use the diamonds for questions to be answered or problems to be solved.	☐
4. I learned how to use circles for yes/no responses.	☐
5. I learned how to use rectangles for actions steps.	☐
6. I learned how to use broken-line rectangles for explanations.	☐
7. I learned how to use trapezoids for answers.	☐
8. I learned how to both construct and interpret flowcharts in social studies.	☐

Comments by Student: _____

_____

_____

Signed _____ Date _____

Comments by Teacher: _____

_____

_____

Signed _____ Date _____

Get the Point Organizer

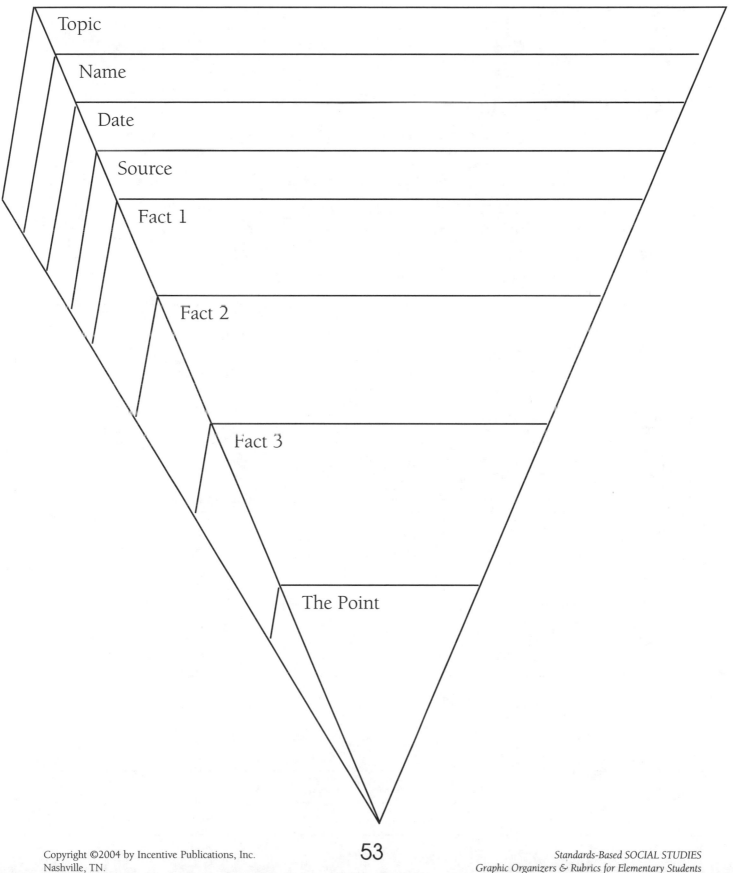

Topic

Name

Date

Source

Fact 1

Fact 2

Fact 3

The Point

Standards-Based SOCIAL STUDIES
Graphic Organizers & Rubrics for Elementary Students

Get the Point Organizer

Rating Scale:

Great   Fair   Needs Work

Directions to Student:

In the triangle at the end of each line, fill in the pyramid to the correct level that shows your work on the activity.

1. I have found the "Get the Point" graphic organizer to be valuable in helping me gather and synthesize information on a given topic.	
2. I have found the topic to be interesting and informative.	
3. I have found the sources of information on the topic to be plentiful, manageable, and varied.	
4. I have found the facts on the topic to be easily translated, summarized, and written up in my own words.	
5. I have found the facts on the topic to culminate in a major point or logical conclusion.	
6. I have found my work on the topic to be both creative and challenging.	

Here are some things I want to remember about this "Get the Point" graphic organizer when I use it again in my future work:

Point One: _____

_____

Point Two: _____

_____

Point Three: _____

_____

Group Project Plan Organizer

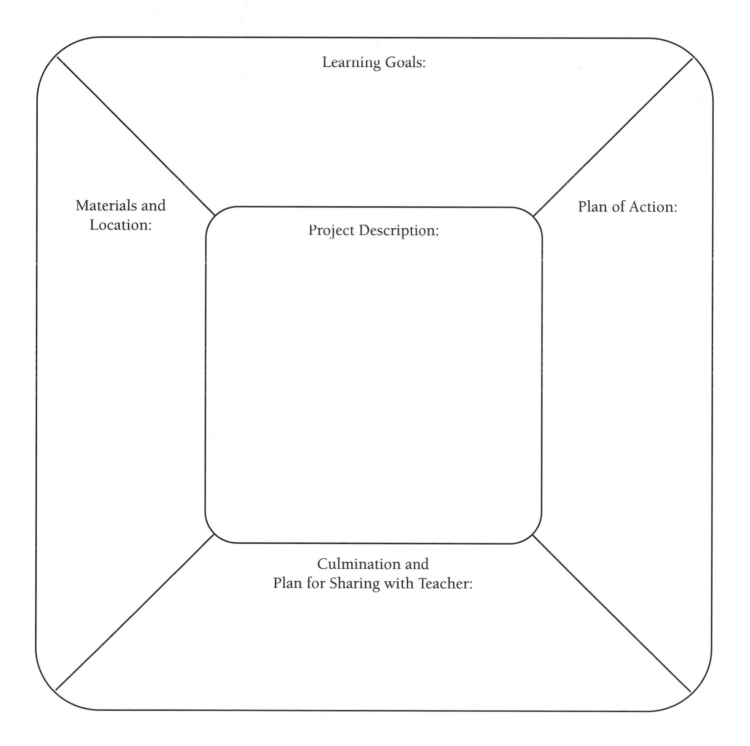

Learning Goals:

Materials and
Location:

Project Description:

Plan of Action:

Culmination and
Plan for Sharing with Teacher:

Group Project Plan Organizer

Rating Scale: Excellent Good Fair Poor

1 2 3 4

Directions to Student:

In the ribbon at the end of each line, write the number that best describes your performance on this activity.

1. QUALITY OF MATERIALS AND LOCATION
   I was able to make a list of the materials I needed
   for my project and where to find them.

2. QUALITY OF LEARNING GOALS
   I was able to write down at least three goals
   to guide my project from start to finish.

3. QUALITY OF PLAN OF ACTION
   I was able to outline the important steps, in sequence,
   for completing my project.

4. QUALITY OF PLAN FOR SHARING WITH TEACHER
   I was able to think of a good way to share the progress
   of my project with my teacher.

Comments by Student: _____

_____

_____

Signed _____ Date _____

Comments by Teacher: _____

_____

_____

Signed _____ Date _____

Group Rating Scale

Activity: _____

	Excellent	Good	Fair	Poor
Group Interaction				
Individual Contributions				
Role Assignments				
Objectives				
Plan of Action				
Materials				
Use of Time				
Overall Rating				

Signatures:

_____   _____

_____   _____

_____   _____

_____   Date: _____

Group Rating Scale

Rating Scale:	1	2	3
	Little Progress	Some Progress	Great Progress

Directions to Student:

In the box at the end of each line, write the number that best describes your work.

1. I understood the nature of the assignment.	☐
2. I had a role to play in completing the task.	☐
3. I adhered to the rules.	☐
4. I made meaningful contributions to the group in achieving group goals.	☐
5. I worked cooperatively and responsibly with members of the group.	☐
6. I practiced active listening skills with group members.	☐
7. I displayed positive and constructive social skills.	☐
8. I assumed responsibility for my actions.	☐
9. I helped to motivate and energize the group to complete tasks.	☐
10. I helped the group plan and implement its activities.	☐

My major contribution to the group's effort was: _____

_____

Something I could do better next time is: _____

_____

Some comments from other members of the group about my performance are:

_____

Questions or remarks for my student/teacher conference:_____

_____

Independent Study Planning Tool

Graphic Organizer

PERSONAL PROJECT PLAN		
Title and Description of Study	Beginning Date _____ Completion Date _____	Format for Study
	Resources Needed and Location	
Challenges to be expected and/or questions to answer		
	Method of Evaluation	

Independent Study Planning Tool

Rating Scale:

1	2	3	4
First Base	Second Base	Third Base	Home Run

Directions to Student:

In the "base" at the end of each line, write the number that best describes your work on the activity.

1. I wrote down a title and a detailed description of my study.	
2. I developed a logical format for my study.	
3. I noted expected challenges and answered key questions.	
4. I succeeded in locating resources and evaluating study results.	

Comments by Student: _____

_____

_____

_____

_____

Signed _____ Date _____

Comments by Teacher: _____

_____

_____

_____

_____

Signed _____ Date _____

Interview Organizer

Getting Ready for the Interview

Name of Interviewee _____

Name of Interviewer _____

Date of Interview _____

Purpose of Interview _____

_____

Conducting the Interview

Question One _____

_____

Response _____

_____

Question Two _____

_____

Response _____

_____

Question Three _____

_____

Response _____

_____

Following the Interview

Results of the Interview _____

_____

_____

_____

Interview Organizer

Rating Scale:

☺   ☻   ☹

Best Work   So-So Work   Not So Good

Directions to Student:

Circle the "face" at the end of each line that best describes your work.

1. I recorded the name of interviewer, name of interviewee, date of interview, and purpose of interview punctually on the organizer sheet.	☺ ☻ ☹
2. I developed a quality set of questions to ask the interviewee during the interview session.	☺ ☻ ☹
3. I used attentive listening skills during the interview.	☺ ☻ ☹
4. I recorded the responses of the interviewee to my questions with accuracy.	☺ ☻ ☹
5. I wrote up the results of the interview using interesting words and correct grammar.	☺ ☻ ☹
6. I learned much about the interview process during this experience.	☺ ☻ ☹

For me, the best part of this interview project was _____

_____

For me, the least successful part of this interview project was _____

_____

For me, the most difficult part of this interview project was _____

_____

For me, the easiest part of this interview project was _____

_____

For me, the thing I would want to do differently next time is _____

_____ because

_____

_____

KWL Organizer

Topic of Study/Title _____

Student's Name _____

What I Know	What I Want to Know	What I Learned

KWL Organizer

Rating Scale:

3	2	1
Know-It-All	Know Some Things	Know-Nothing-At-All

Directions to Student:

In the box at the end of each line, write the number that best describes your work on this activity.

1. I understand the purpose of a KWL Organizer.	☐
2. I understand what the K, W, and L stand for in a KWL Organizer.	☐
3. I understand what to write down in the K column of a KWL Organizer and I was able to do it successfully.	☐
4. I understand what to write down in the W column of a KWL Organizer and I was able to do it successfully.	☐
5. I understand what to write down in the L column of a KWL Organizer and I was able to do it successfully.	☐
6. I understand how a KWL Organizer can help me record, remember, and recall information learned as part of a research or reading task.	☐

This was the most important thing I KNEW about the topic I studied:

_____

_____

This was the most important thing I WANTED to know about the topic I studied:

_____

_____

This was the most important thing I LEARNED about the topic I studied:

_____

_____

Student Signature: _____

Main Idea Map

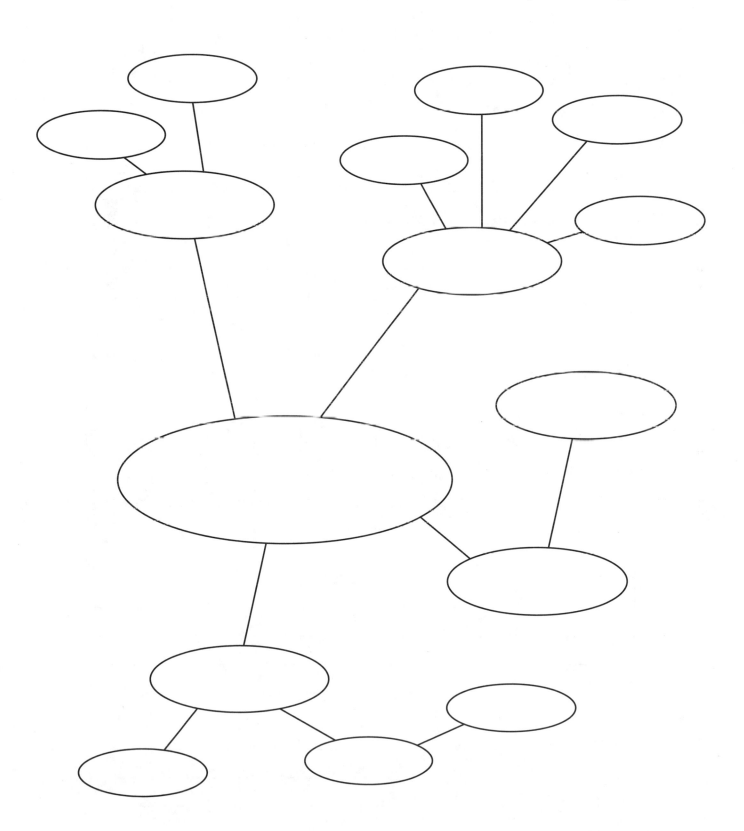

Standards-Based SOCIAL STUDIES
Graphic Organizers & Rubrics for Elementary Students

Main Idea Map

Rating Scale:

    ①   ②   ③

    Excellent   Fair   Poor

Directions to Student:

In the ribbon at the end of each line, write the number that best describes your performance.

1. Quality of my main idea or central concept.	⬤
2. Quality of my sub-topics as related to the main idea or central concept.	⬤
3. Quality of my small ideas as related to the sub-topics.	⬤
4. Quality of my extensions and associations of the main concept in relation to both the sub-topics and the small ideas.	⬤
5. Quality of my lines and circles as drawn on this Main Idea Map.	⬤

Comments by Student: _____

_____

_____

Signed _____ Date _____

Comments by Teacher: _____

_____

_____

Signed _____ Date _____

Observation Log

Graphic Organizer

Date: ______________________ Time: ______________________

Observation: ____

____

____

____

____

____

____

____

____

____

Date: ______________________ Time: ______________________

Observation: ____

____

____

____

____

____

____

____

____

____

Observation Log

Rating Scale:

A	B	C
Absolute Best	Better	Poor

Directions to Student:

In the magnifying glass at the end of each line, write the number that best describes your work.

1. **Appropriateness of Subject:** My subject for the required observations is interesting, important, and manageable.

2. **Quality of my Entries:** My observation entries include important terms, experiences, events, feelings, reactions to observations, summaries, and conclusions on what I see and do.

3. **Details and Descriptions of my Observations:** My observation entries are written using colorful vocabulary and original thought to present details and descriptions in a lively manner.

4. **Grammar:** My observation entries have no errors in grammar or spelling.

5. **Interest:** My observation entries are interesting to read, and hold the reader's attention.

6. **Graphics, Drawings, Sketches:** My observation entries are enhanced with relevant graphics, drawings, or sketches as needed.

Some things I would do differently if I were conducting an observation study again are: _____

_____

_____

_____

Observation Subject: _____

Date Started Observations:_____ Date Completed Observations:_____

Planning Tree Organizer

Planning Tree Organizer

Rating Scale:

1	2	3
Always	Sometimes	Almost Never

Directions to Student:

In the box at the end of each line, write the number that best describes your work.

1. I can explain the purpose of a Planning Tree.	☐
2. I can tell the difference between a major goal and a sub-goal.	☐
3. I can arrange the sequence of tasks in a logical order.	☐
4. I can write all of the major goals in the large boxes.	☐
5. I can write all of the sub-goals in the medium-sized boxes.	☐
6. I can write all of the sequential tasks in the small boxes.	☐
7. I can successfully complete a planning tree for most social studies projects.	☐
8. I find a Planning Tree to be a helpful tool in my work.	☐

Comments by Student: _____

_____

_____

_____

_____

Signed _____ Date _____

Comments by Teacher: _____

_____

_____

_____

_____

Signed _____ Date _____

Pro or Con Chart

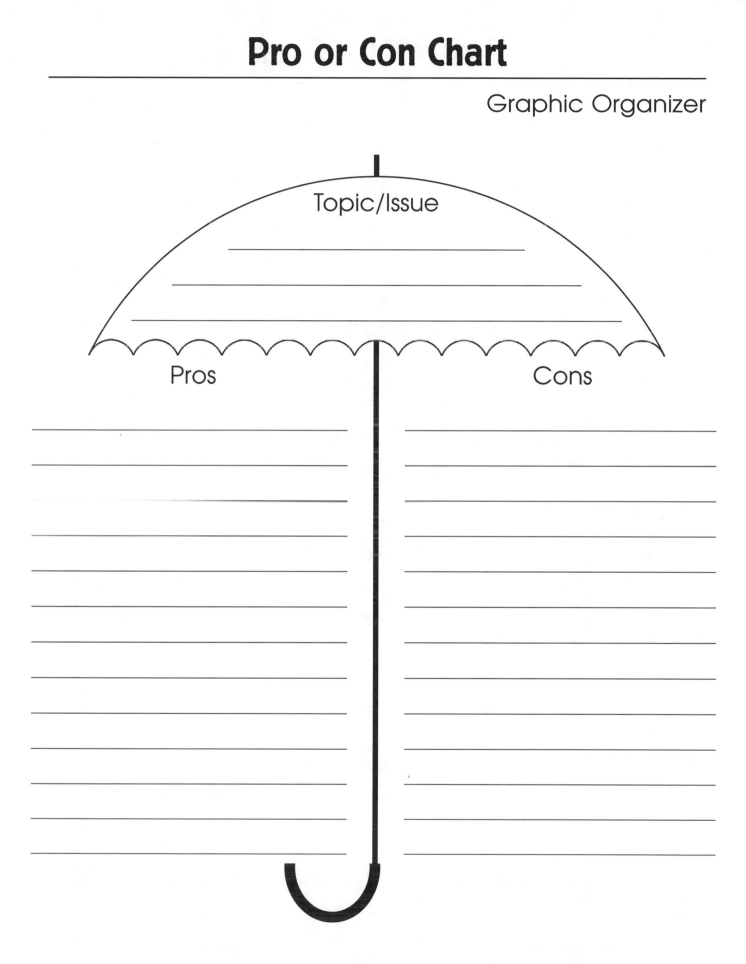

Topic/Issue

_____

_____

_____

Pros   Cons

Pro or Con Chart

Rating Scale:

√+	√	√−
Great Work	Fair Work	Needs Work

Directions to Student/Teacher:

In the box at the end of each line, write the symbol that best describes the work.

	Student	Teacher
1. I did adequate research on my issue/topic.		
2. I found my knowledge of issue/topic to be sufficient for this task.		
3. I was able to identify good pros or arguments for the issue/topic.		
4. I was able to identify good cons or arguments against the issue/topic.		
5. I was able to write down some meaningful conclusions on the issue/topic.		
6. I was able to write down some meaningful solutions on the issue/topic.		

The strongest feature of this Pro or Con Chart is:

Student: _____

Teacher: _____

The weakest feature of this Pro or Con Chart is:

Student: _____

Teacher: _____

Recommendation for improvement on my next Pro or Con Chart is:

Student: _____

Teacher: _____

Problem-Solving Star

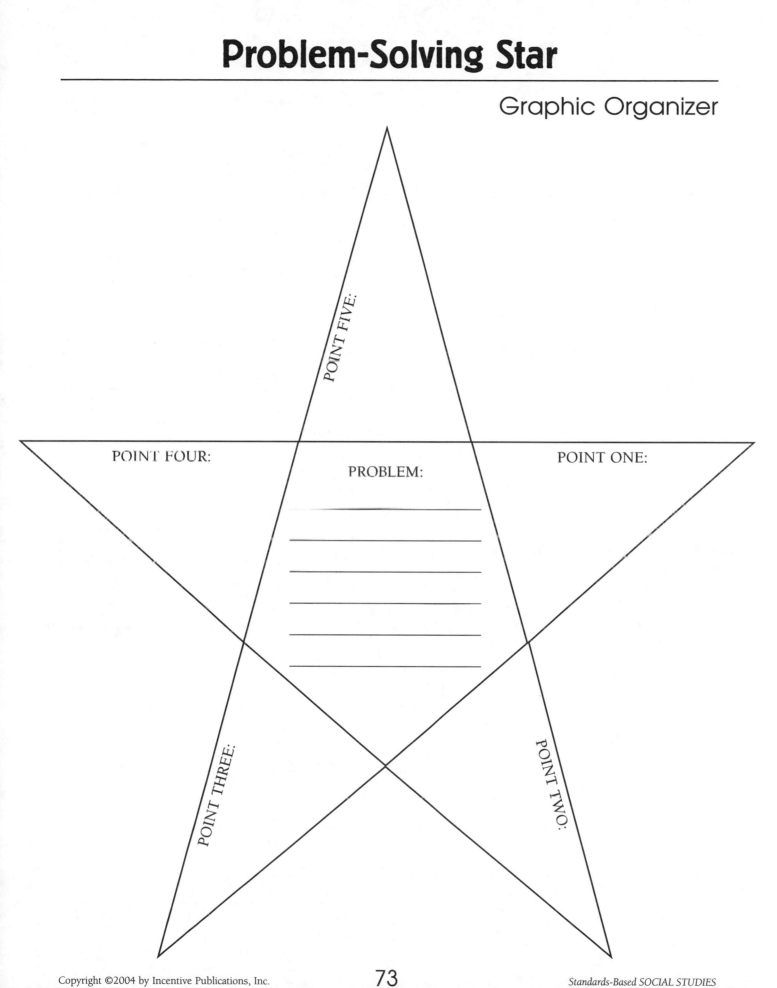

POINT FIVE:

POINT FOUR:

POINT ONE:

PROBLEM:

POINT THREE:

POINT TWO:

Standards-Based SOCIAL STUDIES
Graphic Organizers & Rubrics for Elementary Students

Problem-Solving Star

Rating Scale:

☆ ☆ ★
Novice
Observer

☆ ★ ★
Amateur
Observer

★ ★ ★
Professional
Observer

Directions to Student:

In the box at the end of each line, fill in the number of stars to measure your work.

1. I have selected an interesting problem to study for this assignment.	☆ ☆ ☆
2. I have written the problem statement clearly and grammatically correct in the center of the star.	☆ ☆ ☆
3. I have researched the problem carefully to obtain sufficient information related to the problem.	☆ ☆ ☆
4. I have recorded key points to consider or potential solutions to the problem on the five points of the star.	☆ ☆ ☆
5. I have generated interest in the problem by others who have heard me talk about it.	☆ ☆ ☆
6. I have generated interest in the problem by those who have reviewed my Problem-Solving Star.	☆ ☆ ☆
7. I have learned a great deal about this problem from my work on the assignment.	☆ ☆ ☆

Comments by Student: _____

_____

_____

Signed _____ Date _____

Comments by Teacher: _____

_____

_____

Signed _____ Date _____

Puzzle Pieces Organizer

Topic _____

Student's Name _____ Date _____

75

Puzzle Pieces Organizer

Rating Scale:

Not Pleased	Somewhat Pleased	Very Pleased
☐ ☐ ☐	☐ ■ ■	■ ■ ■

Directions to Student:

Fill in the appropriate number of boxes for your performance on this activity.

1. Quality of my Research Topic	☐ ☐ ☐
2. Quality of my References/Resources	☐ ☐ ☐
3. Quality of my Expressed Opinions	☐ ☐ ☐
4. Quality of my Conclusions	☐ ☐ ☐
5. Quality of my Summaries	☐ ☐ ☐
6. Quality of my Grammar/Spelling	☐ ☐ ☐
7. Quality of my Creative Thinking	☐ ☐ ☐

Comments by Student: _____

_____

_____

_____

_____

Signed _____ Date _____

Comments by Teacher: _____

_____

_____

_____

_____

Signed _____ Date _____

Reading to Learn Record

Section Title	What I Expect to Learn	What I Learned
1.		
2.		
3.		
4.		
5.		
6.		
7.		
8.		
9.		
10.		

Reading to Learn Record

Rating Scale:

A	B	C
Great Understanding: 100–90	Good Understanding: 89–80	Poor Understanding: 79–or below

Directions to Student:

After selecting the chapter in the text, write down the information you wanted to know from each section of the chapter. Then, write down what you learned from the chapter, and rate your overall understanding of the textbook section studied.

Name of Textbook: _____From page ___ to page ____

Chapter Title: _____

Subject: _____

Topic: _____ **MY GRADE** _____

Great Understanding: 100–90

- Can answer questions asked about the text
- Can provide clear and explicit details about the text
- Can supply creative and insightful comments about the text

Good Understanding: 89–80

- Can discuss the text in chronological order and verbalize the highlights
- Can answer most questions asked about the text
- Can provide and discuss details about the text
- Can exhibit understanding of the text's content and intent

Poor Understanding: 79–or below

- Have difficulty discussing the text and/or organizing facts in chronological order
- Can supply few details about the material read
- Have incorrect answers and/or inconsistent answers to questions asked about the text
- Have difficulty verbalizing insights and/or personal reflections related to the text

---

Student Signature _____ Date _____

Teacher Signature _____ Date _____

Scope and Sequence Ladder

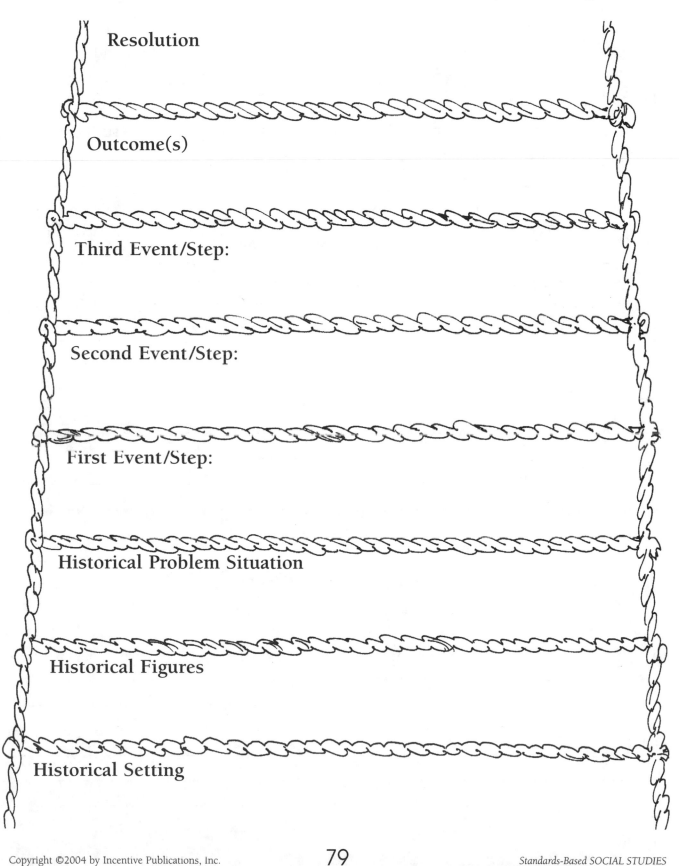

Resolution

Outcome(s)

Third Event/Step:

Second Event/Step:

First Event/Step:

Historical Problem Situation

Historical Figures

Historical Setting

Standards-Based SOCIAL STUDIES
Graphic Organizers & Rubrics for Elementary Students

Scope and Sequence Ladder

Rubric

Rating Scale:	3	2	1
	Does Not Meet Criteria	Average Work	Top of the Ladder

Directions to Student:

In the box at the end of each line, write the number that best describes the quality of your work for each item given.

1. Quality of information on first step of the ladder	☐
2. Quality of information on second step of the ladder	☐
3. Quality of information on third step of the ladder	☐
4. I have summarized the results of the data on this event efficiently.	☐

1. The best step of my ladder is ___ because _____

_____ .

2. The worst step of my ladder is ___ because _____

_____ .

3. The most interesting step of my ladder is ___ because _____

_____ .

4. The least interesting step of my ladder is ___ because _____

_____ .

5. If I were to add a sixth step to my ladder it would probably be _____

_____ .

Comments by Student: _____

_____

_____

Signed _____ Date _____

Comments by Teacher: _____

_____

_____

Signed _____ Date _____

Sequence of Events Map

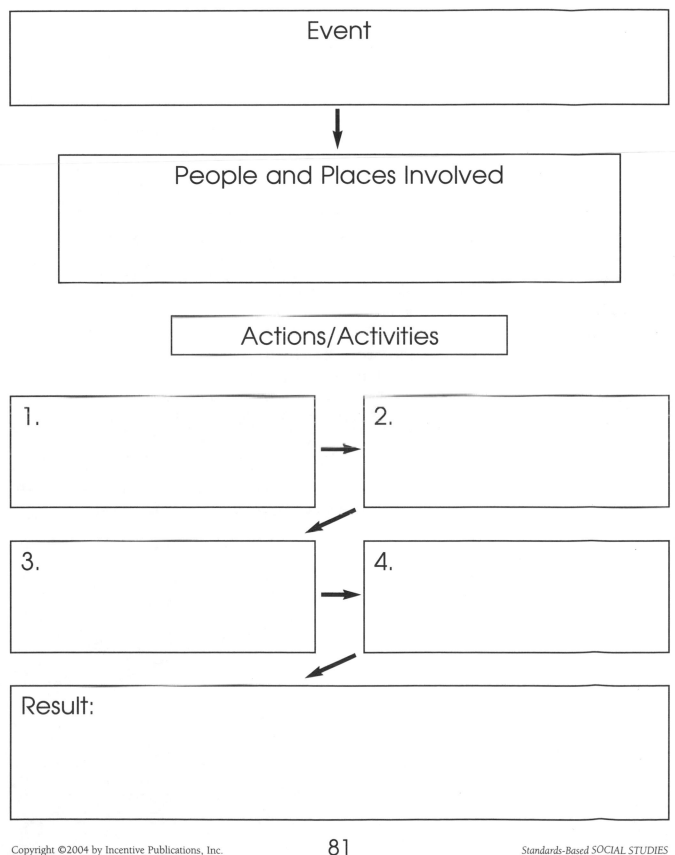

Event

People and Places Involved

Actions/Activities

1.

2.

3.

4.

Result:

Standards-Based SOCIAL STUDIES
Graphic Organizers & Rubrics for Elementary Students

Sequence of Events Map

Rating Scale:

1 ▷ Excellent   2 ▷ Fair   3 ▷ Needs More Work

Directions to Student:

In the flag at the end of each line, write the number that best describes your work.

1. I have chosen an appropriate economic-related event for this activity. ▷

2. I have adequately researched my event. ▷

3. I have identified significant people and places involved in this event. ▷

4. I have reported key pieces of information about the actions and activities associated with this event. ▷

5. I have effectively analyzed the data recorded for this event. ▷

Comments by Student: _____

_____

_____

_____

_____

Signed _____ Date _____

Comments by Teacher: _____

_____

_____

_____

_____

Signed _____ Date _____

Social Studies Homework Helper

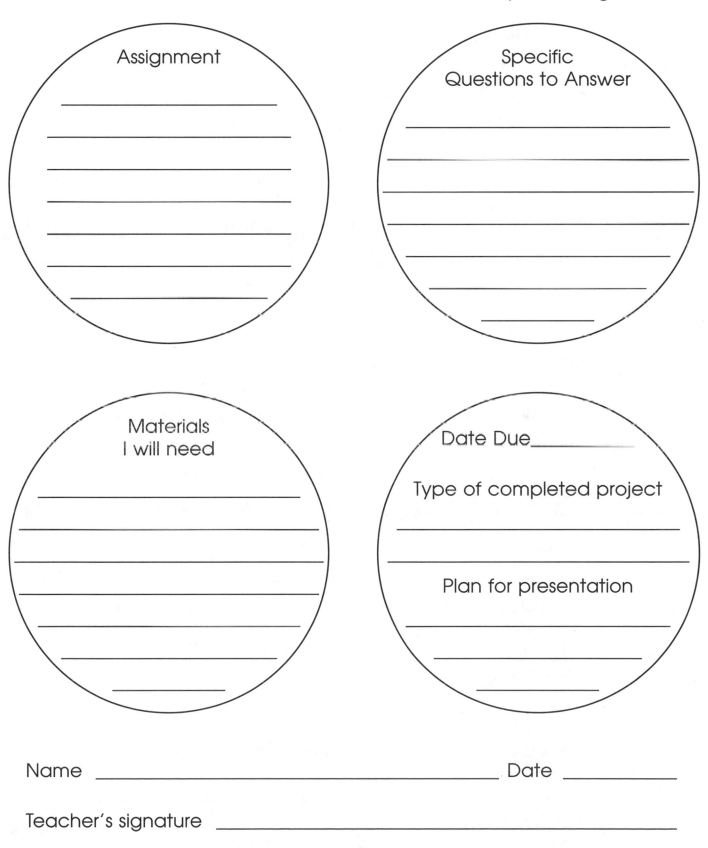

Assignment

_____

_____

_____

_____

_____

_____

Specific
Questions to Answer

_____

_____

_____

_____

_____

Materials
I will need

_____

_____

_____

_____

_____

Date Due_____

Type of completed project

_____

_____

Plan for presentation

_____

_____

_____

Name _____ Date _____

Teacher's signature _____

Standards-Based SOCIAL STUDIES
Graphic Organizers & Rubrics for Elementary Students

Social Studies Homework Helper

Rating Scale: 1   2   3
                 Excellent   Fair   Poor

Directions to Student:

In the box at the end of each line, write the number that best describes your performance on this activity. Otherwise, answer the questions on the lines provided.

1. I was able to write a brief description of project. ☐

2. I was able to generate specific questions to answer. ☐

3. I was able to locate useful materials for this assignment. ☐

4. Major concepts learned from completion of project: _____ _____

5. Main facts learned: _____ _____

6. Skills used during completion of the project: _____ _____

7. New words added to my vocabulary through completion of the project: _____ _____

8. The most difficult part of the project was: _____ _____

9. The most interesting part of the project was: _____ _____

10. The thing I liked best about the project was: _____ _____

11. Meaningfulness of project (circle one)
    (a) Extremely meaningful   (b) Somewhat meaningful   (c) Not very meaningful

12. If I were doing this project again I would: _____ _____

13. When I reflect on the requirement for this project and how I completed it, I would summarize my findings about how I did, what I learned, and its value to me as: _____ _____

14. The grade I feel I deserve for this project is: _____

Storyboard Organizer

Graphic Organizer

1.

6.

2.

7.

3.

8.

4.

9.

5.

10.

Standards-Based SOCIAL STUDIES
Graphic Organizers & Rubrics for Elementary Students

Storyboard Organizer

Rating Scale:

1	2	3
I did well	I did OK	I need to improve

Directions to Student:

Write in each smaller box the number that best describes your work.

1. I was able to describe a series of events in chronological order.

5. I was able to apply a variety of higher order thinking skills in tackling this task.

2. I was able to organize my pieces of information, ideas, thoughts, or situations in a logical sequence based on when and how they occurred.

6. I was able to gain some valuable information on a topic I knew little about.

3. I was able to use this organizer for events leading up to a conflict, war, election, historical moment, discovery, invention, disaster, or exploration.

7. I was able to interest others in the results of my work.

4. I was able to express my ideas using colorful language and correct grammar.

8. I was able to complete my storyboard organizer with little outside help from the teacher.

Comments by Student: _____

_____

Signed _____ Date _____

Comments by Teacher: _____

_____

_____

Signed _____ Date _____

Study Guide for Preparing a Social Studies Project

Topic _____ Date Due _____

I. Description

II. Materials I will need

III. How I will share results

IV. How my project will be assessed

Standards-Based SOCIAL STUDIES
Graphic Organizers & Rubrics for Elementary Students

Study Guide for Preparing a Social Studies Project

Rubric

Rating Scale:

3	2	1
Excellent	Pretty Good	Not So Good

Directions to Student:

In the box at the end of each line, write the number that describes your work on this activity. Then, write a short statement on the blank lines provided about what you did well or what you would do differently next time.

1. My description of the project was accurate, detailed, clearly written, and informative to the reader. ☐

   _____

   _____

   _____

2. My list of materials required for completing the project was complete and on target. ☐

   _____

   _____

   _____

3. My plan for sharing the results of my project was presented in sequential steps and was well received by the audience. ☐

   _____

   _____

   _____

4. My assessment process for judging the quality of my project was manageable and meaningful. ☐

   _____

   _____

   _____

Student Signature _____ Date _____

Teacher Signature _____ Date _____

Study Guide for Preparing for a Social Studies Quiz

Graphic Organizer

1. Major Topics to be covered on the test	2. Sub-Topics

3. Materials to be reviewed (textbooks, class notes, handouts, my own work)	4. Facts to Review

My Study Plan:

1.

2.

3.

4.

5.

6.

7.

8.

Standards-Based SOCIAL STUDIES
Graphic Organizers & Rubrics for Elementary Students

Study Guide for Preparing for a Social Studies Quiz

Rubric

Rating Scale:

3	2	1
I Prepared Well	I Prepared OK	I Failed to Prepare

Directions to Student:

In the box at the end of each line, write the number that best describes your performance on this activity.

1. I was able to identify the major topics to be covered on the quiz. ☐

2. I was able to identify the important sub-topics to be covered on the quiz. ☐

3. I was able to locate and review the key facts/concepts/terms from the textbook to be covered on the quiz. ☐

4. I was able to use my class notes as a tool for covering material on the quiz. ☐

5. I was able to located and review the important teacher/classroom handouts for covering material on the quiz. ☐

6. I was able to organize my own classroom assignment/work as a study guide for covering material on a quiz. ☐

7. I was able to list and prioritize the important facts/concepts/terms to be learned for the quiz. ☐

8. I was able to develop a successful study plan to follow in preparing for the quiz. ☐

Comments by Student: _____

_____

Signed _____ Date _____

Comments by Teacher: _____

_____

Signed _____ Date _____

Standards-Based SOCIAL STUDIES
Graphic Organizers & Rubrics for Elementary Students

Copyright ©2004 by Incentive Publications, Inc.
Nashville, TN.

Surfing the Net Organizer

Graphic Organizer

Directions to Student:

Use the Internet to locate a website where you can find information about each of the different genres in literature that would appeal to kids your age. Record your website in each of the special circles below.

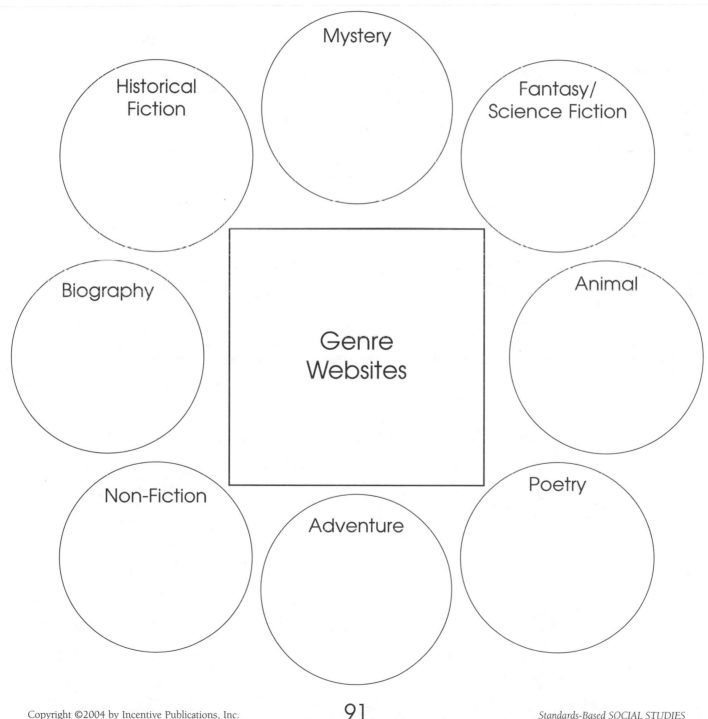

Standards-Based SOCIAL STUDIES
Graphic Organizers & Rubrics for Elementary Students

Surfing the Net Organizer

Rubric

Rating Scale:

3	2	1
Excellent	Fair	Needs Work

Directions to Student:

In the box at the end of each line, write the number that best describes your performance on this activity.

1. I was able to find a website for the poetry genre.	☐
2. I was able to find a website for the adventure genre.	☐
3. I was able to find a website for the fantasy/science fiction genre.	☐
4. I was able to find a website for the animal genre.	☐
5. I was able to find a website for the biography genre.	☐
6. I was able to find a website for the mystery genre.	☐
7. I was able to find a website for the non-fiction genre.	☐
8. I was able to find a website for the historical fiction genre.	☐

Comments by Student: _____

_____

_____

_____

Signed _____ Date _____

Comments by Teacher: _____

_____

_____

_____

Signed _____ Date _____

Venn Diagram

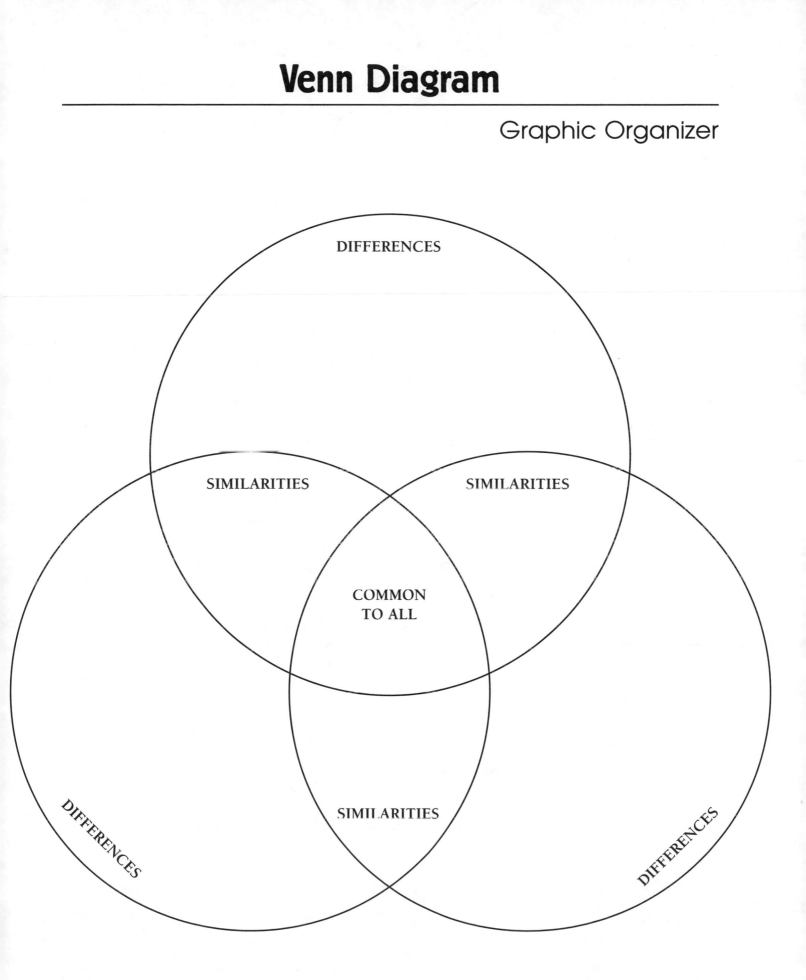

DIFFERENCES

SIMILARITIES

SIMILARITIES

COMMON
TO ALL

DIFFERENCES

SIMILARITIES

DIFFERENCES

Standards-Based SOCIAL STUDIES
Graphic Organizers & Rubrics for Elementary Students

Venn Diagram

Rating Scale:

1	2	3
Maximum Success	Marginal Success	Minimal Success

Directions to Student:

In the box at the end of each line, write the number that best describes your work on this activity.

1. I can explain the use of a Venn Diagram to another person.	☐
2. I can compare and contrast three different (but related) objects, concepts, events, and persons using a Venn Diagram.	☐
3. I can use the intersecting parts of the circles in a Venn Diagram to record the common elements of all three items.	☐
4. I can use the outer parts of the circles in a Venn Diagram to record elements uniquely appropriately for any one of the circles.	☐
5. I can use the intersecting parts of any two circles in a Venn Diagram to record the similar elements of any two items.	☐
6. I can see the value of using a Venn Diagram as a tool for comparison and contrast.	☐

Comments by Student: _____

_____

_____

Signed _____ Date _____

Comments by Teacher: _____

_____

_____

Signed _____ Date _____

What, So What, Now What? Chart

Graphic Organizer

Topic of Study/Title _____

Student's Name _____

What?	So What?	Now What?

Standards-Based SOCIAL STUDIES
Graphic Organizers & Rubrics for Elementary Students

What, So What, Now What? Chart

Rubric

Rating Scale:

Very Good

Good

Not So Good

Directions to Student:

Shade in the number of blocks to show your performance on this activity.

1. I have been able to apply a "What, So What, Now What" pattern to my work. ☐ ☐ ☐

2. I have been able to record a response to the question: "WHAT" is the meaning of this piece and/or what did I learn from it? ☐ ☐ ☐

3. I have been able to record a series of responses to the question: "SO WHAT" difference does it make now that I know this, or what is its importance? ☐ ☐ ☐

4. I have been able to record an answer to the question: "NOW WHAT" can I do to use this information so that it makes a difference in what I know or can do or so I understand how it is important and relates to the major theme of study? ☐ ☐ ☐

Comments by Student: _____

_____

_____

_____

Signed _____ Date _____

Comments by Teacher: _____

_____

_____

_____

Signed _____ Date _____

Standards-Based SOCIAL STUDIES
Graphic Organizers & Rubrics for Elementary Students

Copyright ©2004 by Incentive Publications, Inc.
Nashville, TN.

Williams' Taxonomy Lesson Plan

Graphic Organizer

Theme: _____

	ACTIVITY 1	ACTIVITY 2	ACTIVITY 3
FLUENCY			
FLEXIBILITY			
ORIGINALITY			
ELABORATION			
RISK TAKING			
COMPLEXITY			
CURIOSITY			
IMAGINATION			

NOTE: Not every rectangle needs to be filled in for every topic. However, make sure there is a good content balance in each unit.

Standards-Based SOCIAL STUDIES
Graphic Organizers & Rubrics for Elementary Students

Williams' Taxonomy Lesson Plan

Fluency: Evidence of generating lots of ideas and a large number of choices in a given situation.
___ Great Evidence ___ Ample Evidence ___ Little Evidence

Flexibility: Evidence of altering or redirecting ideas to fit a variety of categories or dimensions in a given situation.
___ Great Evidence ___ Ample Evidence ___ Little Evidence

Originality: Evidence of seeking the unusual by suggesting clever twists to change content or seek the novel in a given situation.
___ Great Evidence ___ Ample Evidence ___ Little Evidence

Elaboration: Evidence of stretching an idea or topic by expanding or embellishing possibilities in order to build on previous thoughts in a given situation.
___ Great Evidence ___ Ample Evidence ___ Little Evidence

Risk Taking: Evidence of dealing with the unknown by taking chances, experimenting with new ideas, or trying new challenges in a given situation.
___ Great Evidence ___ Ample Evidence ___ Little Evidence

Complexity: Evidence of creating structure in an unstructured setting or to bring a logical order to a given situation.
___ Great Evidence ___ Ample Evidence ___ Little Evidence

Curiosity: Evidence of following a hunch, questioning alternatives, pondering outcomes, or wondering about options in a given situation.
___ Great Evidence ___ Ample Evidence ___ Little Evidence

Imagination: Evidence of visualizing possibilities, building images in one's mind, picturing new objects, or reaching beyond the limits of the practical in response to a given situation.
___ Great Evidence ___ Ample Evidence ___ Little Evidence

Comments by Student: _____

_____

Signed _____ Date _____

Comments by Teacher: _____

_____

Signed _____ Date _____

Word Keeper Bookmark

Homework for week of	Homework for week of	Homework for week of	Homework for week of
Subject	Subject	Subject	Subject
Assignment	Assignment	Assignment	Assignment
References/ Textbook pages	References/ Textbook pages	References/ Textbook pages	References/ Textbook pages
Due date	Due date	Due date	Due date
Notes	Notes	Notes	Notes
Grade/Teacher Comments	Grade/Teacher Comments	Grade/Teacher Comments	Grade/Teacher Comments
Student's Name	Student's Name	Student's Name	Student's Name

Standards-Based SOCIAL STUDIES
Graphic Organizers & Rubrics for Elementary Students

Word Keeper Bookmark

Rating Scale:

1   2   3

1st Place   2nd Place   3rd Place

Directions to Student:

Write the number that best describes your work in the ribbon at the end of each line.

1. I have collected many social studies words, terms, phrases, and expressions.	
2. I have researched the definitions and origins of my vocabulary collection.	
3. I have organized my vocabulary collection for future use.	
4. I have used my vocabulary collection in many assignments.	
5. I have recorded my vocabulary collection on my bookmark.	

Comments by Student: _____

_____

Signed _____ Date _____

Comments by Teacher: _____

_____

Signed _____ Date _____

Appendix

Culture

Description

Social studies programs should include experiences that provide for the study of culture and cultural diversity.

Human beings create, learn, and adapt to culture. Culture helps us to understand ourselves both as individual and as members of various groups. Human cultures exhibit both similarities and differences. We all, for example, have systems of beliefs, knowledge, values, and traditions. Each system also is unique. In a democratic and multicultural society, students need to understand multiple perspectives that derive from different cultural vantage points. This understanding will allow them to relate to people in our nation and throughout the world.

Cultures are dynamic and ever-changing. The study of culture prepares students to ask and answer questions such as: What are the common characteristics of different cultures? How do belief systems, such as religion or political ideas of the culture, influence other parts of the culture? How does culture change to accommodate different ideas and beliefs? What does language tell us about culture? In schools, this theme typically appears in units and courses dealing with geography, history, and anthropology, as well as multicultural topics across the curriculum.

In the elementary grades, students begin to explore and ask questions about the nature of culture and specific aspects of culture, such as language and beliefs, and the influence of those aspects on human behavior.

Performance Expectations

Social studies programs should include experiences that provide for the study of culture and cultural diversity so that the elementary learner can:

1. Compare similarities and differences in the ways groups, societies, and cultures meet human needs and concerns.

2. Explain how information and experiences may be interpreted by people from diverse cultural perspectives and frames of reference.

3. Explain and give examples of how language, literature, the arts, architecture, other artifacts, traditions, beliefs, values, and behaviors contribute to the development and transmission of culture.

4. Explain why individuals and groups respond differently to their physical and social environments and/or changes to them on the basis of shared assumptions, values, and beliefs.

5. Articulate the implications of cultural diversity, as well as cohesion within and across groups.

From *Curriculum Standards for Social Studies* as provided by the National Council for Social Studies, Copyright 1994.

Time, Continuity, and Change

Description

Social studies programs should include experiences that provide for the study of how human beings view themselves in and over time.

Human beings seem to understand their historical roots and locate themselves in time. Such understanding involves knowing what things were like in the past and how things will change and develop in the future. Knowing how to read and reconstruct the past allows one to develop a historical perspective and to answer questions such as: Who am I? What happened in the past? How am I connected to those in the past? How has the world changed and how might it change in the future? Why does our personal sense of relatedness to the past change? How can the perspective we have about our own life experiences be viewed as part of the larger human story across time? How do personal stories reflect varying points of view and inform contemporary ideas and actions?

This theme typically appears in courses that: 1) include perspectives from various aspects of history; 2) draw upon historical knowledge during the examination of social issues; and 3) develop the habits of mind that historians and scholars in the humanities and social sciences employ to study the past and its relationship to the present in the United States and other societies.

In the elementary grades, students, through a more formal study of history, continue to expand their understanding of the past and of historical concepts and inquiry. They begin to understand and appreciate differences in historical perspectives, recognizing that interpretations are influenced by individual experiences, societal values, and cultural traditions.

Performance Expectations

Social studies programs should include experiences that provide for the study of the ways human beings view themselves in and over time, so that the elementary grades learner can:

1. Demonstrate an understanding that different scholars may describe the same event or situation in different ways but must provide reasons or evidence for their views.

2. Identify and use key concepts such as chronology, causality, change, conflict, and complexity to explain, analyze, and show connections among patterns of historical change and continuity.

3. Identify and describe selected historical periods and patterns of change within and across cultures, such as the rise of civilizations, the development of transportation systems, the growth and breakdown of colonial systems, and others.

4. Identify and use processes important to reconstructing and reinterpreting the past, such as using a variety of sources, providing, validating, and weighing evidence for claims, checking credibility of sources, and searching for causality.

5. Develop critical sensitivities such as empathy and skepticism regarding attitudes, values, and behaviors of people in different historical contexts.

6. Use knowledge of facts and concepts drawn from history, along with methods of historical inquiry, to inform decision-making about and action-taking on public issues.

From *Curriculum Standards for Social Studies* as provided by the National Council for Social Studies, Copyright 1994.

Standards-Based SOCIAL STUDIES
Graphic Organizers & Rubrics for Elementary Students

People, Places, and Environments

Description

Social studies programs should include experiences that provide for the study of people, places, and environments.

Technological advances connect students at all levels to the world. The study of people, places, and human-environment interactions assists learners as they create their spatial views and geographic perspectives of the world. Today's social, cultural, economic, and civic demands on individuals mean that students will need the knowledge, skills, and understanding to ask and answer questions such as: Where are things located? Why are they located where they are? What patterns are reflected in the groupings of things? What do we mean by region? How do landforms change? What implications do these changes have people? This area of study helps learners make informed and critical decisions about the relationship between human beings and their environment. In schools, this theme typically appears in units and courses dealing with area studies and geography.

During the middle school years, students relate their personal experiences to happenings in environmental contexts. Appropriate experiences will encourage increasingly abstract thought as students use data and apply skills in analyzing human behavior in relation to its physical and cultural environment.

Performance Expectations

Social studies programs should include experiences that provide for the study of people, places, and environments, so that the elementary grades learner can:

1. Elaborate mental maps of locales, regions, and the world that demonstrate understanding of relative location, direction, size, and shape.

2. Create, interpret, use, and distinguish various representations of the earth, such as maps, globes, and photographs.

3. Use appropriate resources, data sources, and geographic tools such as aerial photographs, satellite images, geographic information systems (GIS), map projections, and cartography to generate, manipulate, and interpret information such as atlases, data bases, grid systems, charts, graphs, and maps.

4. Estimate distance, calculate scale, and distinguish other geographic relationships such as population density and spatial distribution patterns.

5. Locate and describe varying landforms and geographic features, such as mountains, plateaus, islands, rain forests, deserts, and oceans, and explain their relationships within the ecosystem.

6. Describe physical system changes such as seasons, climate and weather, and the water cycle and identify geographic patterns associated with them.

7. Describe how people create places that reflect cultural values and ideals as they build neighborhoods, parks, shopping centers, and the like.

8. Examine, interpret, and analyze physical and cultural patterns and their interactions, such as land use, settlement patterns, cultural transmission of customs and ideas, and ecosystem changes.

9. Describe ways that historical events have been influenced by, and have influenced, physical and human geographic factors in local, regional, national, and global settings.

10. Observe and speculate about social and economic effects of environmental changes and crises resulting from phenomena such as floods, storms, and drought.

11. Propose, compare, and evaluate alternative uses of land and resources in communities, regions, nations, and the world.

From *Curriculum Standards for Social Studies* as provided by the National Council for Social Studies, Copyright 1994.

Individual Development and Identity

Description

Social studies programs should include experiences that provide for the study of individual development and identity.

Personal identity is shaped by one's culture, by groups, and by institutional influences. How do people learn? Why do people behave as they do? What influences how people learn, perceive, and grow? How do people meet their basic needs in a variety of contexts? Questions such as these are central to the study of how individuals develop from youth to adulthood. Examination of various forms of human behavior enhances understanding of the relationships among social norms and emerging personal identities, the social processes that influence identity formation, and the ethical principles underlying individual action. In schools, this theme typically appears in units and courses dealing with psychology and anthropology.

Given the nature of individual development and our own cultural context, students need to be aware of the processes of learning, growth, and development at every level of their school experience. In the elementary grades, issues of personal identity are refocused as the individual begins to explain self in relation to others in the society and culture.

Performance Expectations

Social studies programs should include experiences that provide for the study of individual development and identity, so that the elementary grades learner can:

1. Relate personal changes to social, cultural, and historical contexts.
2. Describe personal connections to place—as associated with community, nation, and the world.
3. Describe the ways family, gender, ethnicity, nationality, and institutional affiliations contribute to personal identity.
4. Relate such factors as physical endowment and capabilities, learning, motivation, personality, perception, and behavior to individual development.
5. Identify and describe ways regional, ethnic, and national cultures influence individuals' daily lives.
6. Identify and describe the influence of perception, attitudes, values, and beliefs on personal identity.
7. Identify and interpret examples of stereotyping, conformity, and altruism.
8. Work independently and cooperatively to accomplish goals.

From *Curriculum Standards for Social Studies* as provided by the National Council for Social Studies, Copyright 1994.

Individuals, Groups, and Institutions

Description

    Social studies programs should include experiences that provide for the study of interactions among individuals, groups, and institutions.

    Institutions such as schools, churches, families, government agencies, and the courts all play an integral role in our lives. These and other institutions exert enormous influence over us, yet institutions are no more than organizational embodiments to further the core social values of those who comprise them. Thus, it is important that students know how institutions are formed, what controls and influences them, how they control and influence individuals and culture, and how institutions can be maintained or changed. The study of individuals, groups, and institutions, prepares students to ask and answer questions such as: What is the role of institutions in this and other societies? How am I influenced by institutions? How do institutions change? What is my role in institutional change? In schools, this theme typically appears in units and courses dealing with sociology, anthropology, psychology, political science, and history.

    Elementary grades learners will benefit from varied experiences as they examine the ways in which institutions change over time, promote social conformity, and influence culture. They should be encouraged to use this understanding to suggest ways to work through institutional change for the common good.

Performance Expectations

    Social studies programs should include experiences that provide for the study of interaction among individuals, groups, and institutions, so that the elementary grades learner can:

1. Demonstrate an understanding of concepts such as role, status, and social class in describing the interactions of individuals and social groups.

2. Analyze group and institutional influences on people, events, and elements of culture.

3. Describe the various forms institutions take and the interactions of people with institutions.

4. Identify and analyze examples of tensions between expressions of individuality and group or institutional efforts to promote social conformity.

5. Identify and describe examples of tensions between belief systems and government policies and laws.

6. Describe the role of institutions in furthering both continuity and change.

7. Apply knowledge of how groups and institutions work to meet individual needs and promote the common good.

From *Curriculum Standards for Social Studies* as provided by the National Council for Social Studies, Copyright 1994.

Power, Authority, and Governance

Description

Social studies programs should include experiences that provide for the study of how people create and change structures of power, authority, and governance.

Understanding the historical development of structures of power, authority, and governance and their evolving functions in contemporary U.S. society, as well as in other parts of the world, is essential for developing civic competence. In exploring this theme, students confront questions such as: What is power? What forms does it take? Who holds it? How is it gained, used, and justified? What is legitimate authority? How are governments created, structured, maintained, and changed? How can we keep government responsive to its citizens' needs and interests? How can individual rights be protected within the context of majority rule? By examining the purposes and characteristics of various government systems, learners develop an understanding of how groups and nations attempt to resolve conflicts and seek to establish order and security. Through study of the dynamic relationships among individual rights and responsibilities, the needs of social groups, and concepts of a just society, students become more effective problem-solvers and decision makers when addressing the persistent issues and social problems encountered in public life. They do so buy applying concepts and methods of political science and law. In schools, this theme typically appears in units and courses dealing with government, politics, political science, history, law, and other social sciences.

During the elementary grades years, these rights and responsibilities are applied in more complex contexts with emphasis on new applications. Middle school students should have opportunities to apply their knowledge and skills to and participate in the workings of the various levels of power, authority, and governance.

Performance Expectations

Social studies programs should include experiences that provide for the study of how people create and change structures of power, authority, and governance, so that the elementary grades learner can:

1. Examine persistent issues involving the rights, roles, and status of the individual in relation to the general welfare.
2. Describe the purpose of government and how its powers are acquired, used, and justified.
3. analyze and explain ideas and governmental mechanisms to meet needs and wants of citizens, regulate territory, manage conflict, and establish order and security.
4. Describe the ways nations and organizations respond to forces of unity and diversity affecting order and security.
5. Identify and describe the basic features of the political system in the United States, and identify representative leaders from various levels and branches of government.
6. Explain conditions, actions, and motivations that contribute to conflict and cooperation within and among nations.
7. Describe and analyze the role of technology in communications, transportation, information processing, weapons development, or other areas as they contribute to or help resolve conflicts.
8. Explain and apply concepts such as power, role, status, justice, and influence to the examination of persistent issues and social problems.
9. Give examples and explain how governments attempt to achieve their stated ideals at home and abroad.

From *Curriculum Standards for Social Studies* as provided by the National Council for Social Studies, Copyright 1994.

Production, Distribution, and Consumption

Description

Social studies programs should include experiences that provide for the study of how people organize for the production, distribution, and consumption of goods and services.

People have wants that often exceed the limited resources available to them. As a result, a variety of ways have been invented to decide upon answers to four fundamental questions: What is to be produced? How is production to be organized? How are goods and services to be distributed? What is the most effective allocation of the factors of production (land, labor, capital, and management)? Unequal distribution of resources necessitates systems of exchange, including trade, to improve the well-being of the economy, while the role of government in economic policymaking varies over time and from place to place. Increasingly these decisions are global in scope and require systematic study of an interdependent world economy and the role of technology in economic decision-making. In schools, this theme typically appears in units and courses dealing with concepts, principles, and issues drawn from the discipline of economics.

In the elementary grades, learners expand their knowledge of economic concepts and principles, and use economic reasoning processes in addressing issues related to the four fundamental economic questions.

Performance Expectations

Social studies programs should include experiences that provide for the study of how people organize for the production, distribution, and consumption of goods and services, so that the elementary grades learner can:

1. Give and explain examples of ways that economic systems structure choices about how goods and services are to be produced and distributed.

2. Describe the role that supply and demand, prices, incentives, and profits play in determining what is produced and distributed in a competitive market system.

3. Explain the difference between private and public goods and services.

4. Describe a range of examples of the various institutions that make up economic systems such as households, business firms, banks, government agencies, labor unions, and corporations.

5. Describe the role of specialization and exchange in the economic process.

6. Explain and illustrate how values and beliefs influence different economic decisions.

7. Differentiate among various forms of exchange and money.

8. Compare basic economic systems according to who determined what is produced, distributed, and consumed.

9. Use economic concepts to help explain historical and current developments and issues in local, national, or global contexts.

10. Use economic reasoning to compare different proposals for dealing with a contemporary social issue such as unemployment, acid rain, or high quality education.

From *Curriculum Standards for Social Studies* as provided by the National Council for Social Studies, Copyright 1994.

Science, Technology, and Society

Description

Social studies programs should include experiences that provide for the study of relationships among science, technology, and society.

Technology is as old as the first crude tool invented by prehistoric humans, but today's technology forms the basis for some of our most difficult social choices. Modern life as we know it would be impossible without technology and the science that supports it. But technology brings with it many questions: Is new technology always better than that which it will replace? What can we learn from the past about how new technologies result in broader social change, some of which is unanticipated? How can we cope with the ever-increasing pace of change, perhaps even with the feeling that technology has gotten out of control? How can we manage technology so that the greatest number of people benefit from it? How can we preserve our fundamental values and beliefs in a world that is rapidly becoming one technology-linked village? This theme appears in units or courses dealing with history, geography, economics, and civics and government. It draws upon several scholarly fields from the natural and physical sciences, social sciences, and the humanities for specific examples of issues and the knowledge base for considering responses to the societal issues related to science and technology.

By the elementary grades, students can begin to explore the complex relationships among technology, human values, and behavior. They will find that science and technology bring changes that surprise us and even challenge our beliefs, as in the case of discoveries and their applications related to our universe, the genetic basis of life, atomic physics, and others.

Performance Expectations

Social studies programs should include experiences that provide for the study of relationships among science, technology, and society, so that the elementary grades learner can:

1. Examine and describe the influence of culture on scientific and technological choices and advancement, such as in transportation, medicine, and warfare.

2. Show through specific examples how science and technology have changed people's perceptions of the social and natural world, such as in their relationship to the land, animal life, family life, and economic needs, wants, and security.

3. Describe examples in which values, beliefs, and attitudes have been influenced by new scientific and technological knowledge, such as the invention of the printing press, conceptions of the universe, applications of atomic energy, and genetic discoveries.

4. Explain the need for laws and policies to govern scientific and technological applications, such as in the safety and well-being of workers and consumers and the regulation of utilities, radio, and television.

5. Seek reasonable and ethical solutions to problems that arise when scientific advancements and social norms or values come into conflict.

From *Curriculum Standards for Social Studies* as provided by the National Council for Social Studies, Copyright 1994.

Standards-Based SOCIAL STUDIES
Graphic Organizers & Rubrics for Elementary Students

Global Connections

Description

Social studies programs should include experiences that provide for the study of global connections and interdependence.

The realities of global interdependence require understanding the increasingly important and diverse global connections among world societies. Analysis of tensions between national interests and global priorities contributes to the development of possible solutions to persistent and emerging global issues in many fields: health care, economic development, environmental quality, universal human rights, and others. Analyzing patterns and relationships within and among world cultures, such as economic development, environmental quality, universal human rights, and others. Analyzing patterns and relationships within and among world cultures, such as economic competition and interdependence, age-old ethnic enmities, political and military allowances, and others, helps learners carefully examine policy alternatives that have both national and global implications. This theme typically appears in units or courses dealing with geography, culture, and economics, but again can draw upon the natural and physical sciences and the humanities, including literature, the arts, and language.

In the elementary grades, learners can initiate analysis of the interactions among states and nations and their cultural complexities as they respond to global events and changes.

Performance Expectations

Social studies programs should include experiences that provide for the study of global connections and interdependence, so that the elementary grades learner can:

1. Describe instances in which language, art, music, belief systems, and other cultural elements can facilitate global understanding or cause misunderstanding.

2. Analyze examples of conflict, cooperation, and interdependence among groups, societies, and nations.

3. Describe and analyze the effects of changing technologies on the global community.

4. Explore the causes, consequences, and possible solutions to persistent, contemporary, and emerging global issues, such as health, security, resource allocation, economic development, and environmental quality.

5. Describe and explain the relationships and tensions between national sovereignty and global interests, in such matters as territory, natural resources, trade, use of technology, and welfare of people.

6. Demonstrate understanding of concerns, standards, issues, and conflicts related to universal human rights.

7. Identify and describe the roles of international and multinational organizations.

From *Curriculum Standards for Social Studies* as provided by the National Council for Social Studies, Copyright 1994.

Civic Ideals and Practices

Description

Social studies programs should include experiences that provide for the study of the ideals, principles, and practices of citizenship in a democratic republic.

An understanding of civic ideals and practices of citizenship is critical to full participation in society and is a central purpose of the social studies. All people have a stake in examining civic ideals and practices in diverse societies. Learners confront such questions as: What is civic participation and how can I be involved? How has the meaning of citizenship evolved? What is the balance between rights and responsibilities? What is the role of the citizen in the community and the nation, and as a member of the world community? How can I make a positive difference? In schools, this theme typically appears in units or courses dealing with history, political science, cultural anthropology, and fields such as global studies and law-related education, while also drawing upon content from the humanities.

By the elementary grades, students expand their ability to analyze and evaluate the relationships between ideals and practice. They are able to see themselves taking civic roles in their communities.

Performance Expectations

Social studies programs should include experiences that provide for the study of the ideals, principles, and practices of citizenship in a democratic republic, so that the elementary grades learner can:

1. Examine the origins and continuing influence of key ideals of the democratic republican form of government, such as individual human dignity, liberty, justice, equality, and the rule of law.

2. Identify and interpret sources and examples of the rights and responsibilities of citizens.

3. Locate, access, analyze, organize, and apply information about selected public issues—recognizing and explaining multiple points of view.

4. Practice forms of civic discussion and participation consistent with the ideals of citizens in a democratic republic.

5. Explain and analyze various forms of citizen action that influence public policy decisions.

6. Identify and explain the roles of formal and informal political actors in influencing and shaping public policy and decision-making.

7. Analyze the influence of diverse forms of public opinion on the development of public policy and decision-making.

8. Analyze the effectiveness of selected public policies and citizen behaviors in realizing the stated ideals of a democratic republican form of government.

9. Explain the relationship between policy statements and action plans used to address issues of public concern.

10. Examine strategies designed to strengthen the "common good," which consider a range of options for citizen action.

From *Curriculum Standards for Social Studies* as provided by the National Council for Social Studies, Copyright 1994.

Planning Matrix

Correlatives: National Social Studies Standards as identified by the National Council of Social Studies with activities and projects in Standards-Based Social Studies Graphic Organizers & Rubrics for Elementary Students, Incentive Publications, 2004.

Standards	Graphic Organizers	Rubrics
Culture	29, 31, 37, 39, 47, 53, 55, 65, 69, 81, 93	30, 32, 38, 40, 48, 54, 56, 66, 70, 82, 94
Time Continuity & Change	29, 31, 37, 41, 47, 51, 53, 65, 71, 79, 81, 85, 95	30, 32, 38, 42, 48, 52, 54, 56, 66, 72, 80, 82, 86, 96
People, Places, & Environments	29, 31, 37, 39, 45, 47, 49, 53, 55, 61, 65, 93, 97	30, 32, 38, 40, 46, 48, 50, 54, 56, 62, 66, 94, 98

Planning Matrix

Correlatives: National Social Studies Standards as identified by the National Council of Social Studies with activities and projects in Standards-Based Social Studies Graphic Organizers & Rubrics for Elementary Students, Incentive Publications, 2004.

Standards	Graphic Organizers	Rubrics
Individual Development & Identity	29, 31, 37, 43, 47, 49, 53, 55, 59, 61, 63, 73, 77, 83, 87, 89, 95, 99	30, 32, 38, 44, 48, 50, 54, 56, 60, 62, 64, 74, 78, 84, 88, 90, 96, 100
Individual Groups & Institutions	29, 31, 37, 43, 47, 49, 53, 55, 57, 93	30, 32, 38, 44, 48, 50, 54, 56, 58, 94
Power, Authority, & Governance	29, 31, 33, 35, 37, 47, 53, 55	30, 32, 34, 36, 38, 48, 54, 56

Planning Matrix

Correlatives: National Social Studies Standards as identified by the National Council of Social Studies with activities and projects in Standards-Based Social Studies Graphic Organizers & Rubrics for Elementary Students, Incentive Publications, 2004.

Standards	Graphic Organizers	Rubrics
Production, Distribution, & Consumption	29, 31, 37, 47, 51, 53, 55, 65, 69, 75, 79, 85	30, 32, 38, 48, 52, 54, 56, 65, 70, 76, 80, 86
Science, Technology, & Society	29, 31, 37, 47, 53, 55, 65, 67, 79, 85, 91	30, 32, 38, 48, 54, 56, 66, 68, 80, 86, 92
Global Connections	37, 47, 49, 51, 6, 75, 79, 85, 91, 93, 95	38, 48, 50, 52, 66, 76, 80, 86, 92, 94, 96
Civic Ideals & Practices	29, 31, 33, 37, 47, 53, 55, 57, 65, 71, 77	30, 32, 34, 38, 48, 54, 56, 58, 66, 72, 78

Standards-Based SOCIAL STUDIES
Graphic Organizers & Rubrics for Elementary Students

GUIDELINES
For Using Graphic Organizers

1. Graphic organizers can be used for curriculum planning, helping students process information, and as pre- or post-assessment tasks. Determine which types of graphic organizers are best for each purpose.

2. Graphic organizers are a performance-based model of assessment and make excellent artifacts for inclusion in a student portfolio. Decide which concepts in your discipline are best represented by the use of these organizers.

3. Use graphic organizers to help students focus on important concepts while omitting extraneous details.

4. Use graphic organizers as visual pictures to help the student remember key ideas.

5. Use graphic organizers to connect visual language with verbal language in active learning settings.

6. Use graphic organizers to enhance recall of important information.

7. Use graphic organizers to provide student motivation and relieve student boredom.

8. Use graphic organizers to show and explain relationships between and among varied content areas.

9. Use graphic organizers to make traditional lesson plans more interactive and more appealing to the visual learner.

10. Use graphic organizers to break down complex ideas through concise and structured visuals.

11. Use graphic organizers to help students note patterns and clarify ideas.

12. Use graphic organizers to help students better understand the concept of "part to whole."

13. Emphasize the use of graphic organizers to stimulate creative thinking.

14. Make sure there is a match between the type of organizer and the content being taught.

15. Make sure that using a graphic organizer is the best use of time when teaching a concept.

16. Use a wide variety of graphic organizers and use them collaboratively whenever possible.

GUIDELINES
for Using Rubrics

1. The rubric reflects the most important elements of an assigned task, product, or performance and enables both student and teacher to depict accurately the level of competence or stage of development of individual students.

2. The rubric is planned to augment, reinforce, personalize, and strengthen (but not replace) the assessment program mandated by curriculum guidelines or system requirements.

3. The rubric encourages student self-evaluation and can be shared with students prior to beginning the task so that students know exactly what represents quality work.

4. The rubric has two components which are: (1) characteristics or criteria for quality work on a specific task, and (2) determination of the specific levels of proficiency or degrees of success for each part of a task.

5. The rubric is designed to explain more concretely what a child knows and can do and is less subjective and more focused than other means of student evaluation.

6. Rating scales have been created to evaluate student performance. Easy-to-use weights for each answer make the results clear and specific.

7. If the rubric is holistic, it consists of paragraphs arranged in a hierarchy so that each level of proficiency has a paragraph describing factors that would result in that specific level.

8. If the rubric is analytical, it consists of a listing of criteria most characteristic of that task accompanied with the degrees of success for each model listed separately beside or under each criterion.

9. Samples of student work have been studied to determine realistic attributes common to varied performances at different levels of proficiency. These attributes have been translated into descriptors for the degrees of proficiency and to establish a rating scale to delineate those degrees of proficiency.

10. The rubric is accompanied by carefully planned opportunities for meta-cognitive reflections to provide for self-assessment observations completely unique to the students' own learning goals, expectations, and experiences.

The Graphic Organizer Report Assessment

Rubric

Rating Scale: = High flyer   = Airborne   = Grounded

---

1. **Quality of Report Format:**
   The graphic organizer selected is an appropriate choice for use in the report.   Rating: _____

2. **Quality of Information:**
   The information shows significant research on the topic.   Rating: _____

3. **Grammar:**
   Spelling, grammar, and punctuation have been checked carefully.   Rating: _____

4. **Interest:**
   The different subtopics fit together well and highlight the main points of the topic.   Rating: _____

5. **Graphics/Creativity:**
   The graphic organizer fits the information to be organized and is used in a unique and/or creative way to convey the information as efficiently as possible.   Rating: _____

Comments by Student: _____

_____

_____

Signed _____ Date _____

Comments by Teacher: _____

_____

_____

Signed _____ Date _____

Overall Rating: _____

Signed _____ Date _____

Standards-Based SOCIAL STUDIES
Graphic Organizers & Rubrics for Elementary Students

Calendar for Use of Graphic Organizers

	Monday	Tuesday	Wednesday	Thursday	Friday
Knowledge/ Comprehension	Use magazines, newspapers, and your textbooks to find a wide assortment of graphic organizers. State the main purpose or type of information given in each graphic organizer.	List all the different ways you can think of that we use graphic organizers in our everyday lives. Consider how they are used in department stores, in airports, in supermarkets, and in sports.	Define graphic organizers using your own words, then use a dictionary. Compare the two definitions.	Take the information in one of the graphic organizers and rewrite it in another form.	Classify your collection of graphic organizers in at least three different ways. Explain the rationale for your grouping.
Comprehension/ Application/ Analysis	Compare a chart and a table. In a good paragraph, summarize how they are alike and how they are different.	Collect information about junk foods popular with your age group. Use a Venn Diagram to show your results.	Construct a flowchart to show how you would like to spend a perfect 24-hour day.	Survey the students in your class to determine their favorite television show. Show your results on a graphic organizer.	How is a graphic organizer like a road map? Like a blueprint? Like a photograph?
Analysis/ Synthesis	Study your collection of graphic organizers. Determine some types of data and subject matter that are best depicted by a graphic organizer.	Diagram a flowchart for constructing a graph or a table on grade point averages for students in your language arts class.	Write a story that has one of the following titles: "The Magic Web" "Who Needs a Concept Map?" "Who Moved My Graphic Organizer?"	Draw a picture or write a paragraph to illustrate one of these expressions: "He turned the tables on me!" "It's time to chart your course!"	Design a poster about a school project, event, or activity that uses a graphic organizer as part of its message.
Evaluation	Develop a set of recommendations for students to follow when constructing a high-quality graphic organizer.	Develop a set of criteria for judging the worth or value of a given graphic organizer. Apply this criteria to each unit of your collection. Rank order your graphic organizers, from most effective to least effective.	Defend this statement: Presenting a graphic organizer is the best way to convince a friend of something.	Design a poster of graphic organizers. Find as many different examples as you can. Mount examples on poster board and write three insightful questions about each one.	Explain how each of the following people might use graphic organizers in their work: computer programmer, teacher, mall manager, astronaut, brain surgeon, and carpenter.

Standards-Based SOCIAL STUDIES
Graphic Organizers & Rubrics for Elementary Students

Gardner's Multiple Intelligences

Did you know there are eight different types of intelligence and that each of us possesses all eight, although one or more of them may be stronger than others? Dr. Howard Gardner, a researcher and professor at the Harvard Graduate School of Education, developed the Theory of Multiple Intelligences to help us better understand ourselves and the way we acquire information in school.

Try to rank order the eight intelligences below as they best describe the way *you* learn, with "1" being your weakest intelligence area and "8" being your strongest intelligence area. Try to think of examples and instances in the classroom when you were successful on a test, assignment, activity, or task because it was compatible with the way you like to learn.

_____ 1. **Linguistic Intelligence:** Do you find it easy to memorize information, write poems or stories, give oral talks, read books, play word games like Scrabble and Password, use big words in your conversations or assignments, and remember what you hear?

_____ 2. **Logical/Mathematical Intelligence:** Do you find it easy to compute numbers in your head and on paper, to solve brain teasers, to do logic puzzles, to conduct science experiments, to figure out number and sequence patterns, and to watch videos or television shows on science and nature themes?

_____ 3. **Spatial Intelligence:** Do you find it easy to draw, paint, or doodle, work through puzzles and mazes, build with blocks or various types of buildings sets, follow maps and flowcharts, use a camera to record what you see around you, and prefer reading material with many illustrations?

_____ 4. **Bodily/Kinesthetic Intelligence:** Do you find it easy to engage in lots of sports and physical activities, move around rather than sit still, spend free time outdoors, work with your hands on such things as model-building or sewing, participate in dance, ballet, gymnastics, plays, puppet shows or other performances, and mess around with finger painting, clay, and papier-mâché?

_____ 5. **Musical Intelligence:** Do you find it easy to play a musical instrument or sing in the choir, listen to favorite records or tapes, make up your own songs or raps, recognize off-key recordings or noises, remember television jingles and lyrics of many different songs, and work while listening to or humming simple melodies and tunes?

_____ 6. **Interpersonal Intelligence:** Do you find it easy to make friends, meet strangers, resolve conflicts among peers, lead groups or clubs, engage in gossip, participate in team sports, plan social activities, and teach or counsel others?

_____ 7. **Intrapersonal Intelligence:** Do you find it easy to function independently, do your own work and thinking, spend time alone, engage in solo hobbies and activities, attend personal growth seminars, set goals, analyze your own strengths and weaknesses, and keep private diaries or journals?

_____ 8. **Naturalist Intelligence:** Do you find yourself extremely comfortable and happy outdoors, have a desire to explore and observe the environment, use outdoor equipment such as binoculars easily, and want to understand how natural systems evolve and how things work?

Standards-Based SOCIAL STUDIES
Graphic Organizers & Rubrics for Elementary Students

Bloom's Taxonomy of Cognitive Thinking Skills

Bloom's Taxonomy of Cognitive Thinking Skills is a model that can help you learn how to think critically and systematically. (*Taxonomy* is another word for *structure* or *schemata*.) This taxonomy provides a way to organize thinking skills into six levels. The first level is the most basic, or simplest, level of thinking, and the last level is the most challenging, or most complex, level of thinking.

KNOWLEDGE LEVEL:

Students thinking at this level are asked to memorize, remember, and recall previously learned material. Some common verbs or behaviors for this level are: define, list, identify, label, name, recall, record, draw, recite, and reproduce.

COMPREHENSION LEVEL:

Students thinking at this level are asked to demonstrate their ability to understand the meaning of material learned and to express that meaning in their own words. Some common verbs or behaviors for this level are: explain, describe, summarize, give examples, classify, find, measure, prepare, re-tell, reword, rewrite, and show.

APPLICATION LEVEL:

Students thinking at this level are asked to use learned material in a situation different from the situation in which the material was taught. Some common verbs or behaviors for this level are: apply, compute, construct, develop, discuss, generalize, interview, investigate, model, perform, plan, present, produce, prove, solve, and use.

ANALYSIS LEVEL:

Students thinking at this level are asked to break down material (ideas and concepts) into its component parts so that the organization and relationships between parts is better recognized and understood. Some common verbs or behaviors for this level are: compare and contrast, criticize, debate, determine, diagram, differentiate, discover, draw conclusions, examine, infer, search, survey, and sort.

SYNTHESIS LEVEL:

Students thinking at this level are asked to put together parts of the material to form a new and different whole. Synthesis is the exact opposite of analysis. Some common verbs or behaviors for this level are: build, combine, create, design, imagine, invent, make-up, produce, propose, and present.

EVALUATION LEVEL:

Students thinking at this level are asked to judge the value of material (a statement, novel, poem, research finding, fact) for a given purpose. All judgments are to be based on a set of clearly defined criteria whose outcomes can be defended or validated. Some common verbs or behaviors for this level are: assess, critique, defend, evaluate, grade, judge, measure, rank, recommend, select, test, validate, and verify.

Criteria for Creating Your Own Rubric

Excellent

My portfolio, project, or task
1. is complete.
2. is well-organized.
3. is visually exciting.
4. shows much evidence of multiple resources.
5. shows much evidence of problem solving, decision making, and higher-order thinking skills.
6. reflects enthusiasm for the subject.
7. contains additional work beyond the requirements.
8. communicates effectively what I have learned in keeping with my learning objectives.
9. includes highly efficient assessment tools and makes ample provisions for meta cognitive reflection.
10. has identified many future learning goals in keeping with my own needs and interests.

Good

My portfolio, project, or task
1. is complete.
2. is well-organized.
3. is interesting.
4. shows some evidence of multiple resources.
5. shows some evidence of problem solving, decision making, and higher-order thinking skills.
6. reflects some interest for the topic.
7. contains a small amount of work beyond the requirements.
8. communicates some things I have learned in keeping with my learning objectives.
9. includes effective assessment tools and reflective comments.
10. has identified some future learning goals in keeping with my own needs and interests.

Needs Improvement

My portfolio, project, or task
1. is incomplete.
2. is poorly organized.
3. is not very interesting to others.
4. shows little or almost no evidence of multiple resources.
5. shows little or almost no evidence of problem solving, decision making, and higher-order thinking skills.
6. reflects little interest in the subject.
7. contains no additional work beyond the minimum requirements.
8. communicates few things that I have truly learned in keeping with my objectives.
9. includes few examples of self assessment tools and reflective comments.
10. has identified no future learning goals in keeping with my own needs and interests.

Performance, Project, or Task
Independent Study Contract

Title _____

Topic _____

Beginning date of work_____

Planned completion/delivery date _____

Goals and/or learning objectives to be accomplished_____
_____

Statement of problems to be researched/studied _____
_____

Format _____

Information/data/resources needed _____
_____

Technical help needed_____
_____

Special equipment and/or materials needed _____
_____

Visual aids and/or artifacts planned_____
_____

Intended audience_____

Method of assessment_____

Student Signature _____ Date: _____

Teacher Signature _____ Date: _____

Williams' Taxonomy
of Creative Thought

FLUENCY

Enables the learner to generate a great many ideas, related answers, or choices in a given situation.
> *Sample Cue Words: Generating oodles, lots, many ideas.*

FLEXIBILITY

Lets the learner change everyday objects to generate a variety of categories by taking detours and varying sizes, shapes, quantities, time limits, requirements, objectives, or dimensions in a given situation.
> *Sample Cue Words: Generating varied, different, alternative ideas.*

ORIGINALITY

Causes the learner to seek new ideas by suggesting unusual twists to change content or by coming up with clever responses to a given situation.
> *Sample Cue Words: Generating unusual, unique, new ideas.*

ELABORATION

Helps the learner stretch by expanding, enlarging, enriching, or embellishing possibilities that build on previous thoughts or ideas.
> *Sample Cue Words: Generating enriched, embellished, expanded ideas.*

RISK TAKING

Enables the learner to deal with the unknown by taking chances, experimenting with new ideas, or trying new challenges.
> *Sample Cue Words: Experimenting with and exploring ideas.*

COMPLEXITY

Permits the learner to create structure in an unstructured setting or to build a logical order in a given situation.
> *Sample Cue Words: Improving and explaining ideas.*

CURIOSITY

Encourages the learner to follow a hunch, question alternatives, ponder outcomes, and wonder about options in a given situation.
> *Sample Cue Words: Pondering and questioning ideas.*

IMAGINATION

Allows the learner to visualize possibilities, build images in his or her mind, picture new objects, or reach beyond the limits of the practical.
> *Sample Cue Words: Visualizing and fantasizing ideas.*

Suggestions for Using Graphic Organizers to Integrate Social Studies into the Total Curriculum

1. Use concept webs or other advanced organizers to explain scientific ideas as they relate to historical events or current happenings.
   Example: Give a speech on pollution or endangered species.

2. Construct flowcharts or diagrams to show processes for completing a specific task related to gathering and disseminating facts and/or information about a social issue of concern to people of your age. *Example:* Use a flowchart to plan and develop a research project on a political or economic concern related to conserving our natural resources for the next generation.

3. Design a puppet show storyboard that shows parts of an important event currently affecting global peace, national security, political stability, or some other topic of social significance. Remember that a storyboard does not attempt to show all of the scenes in a story, but merely serves as an outline for the major people, places, and events.

4. Design a explanatory chart to show an audience the relationships, sequences, or positions that exist within an institution, group, or collection of data. Consider any topic for this chart, from the organization of the various branches of military services, to the types of food chains in natural habitats, to the interactions of fictional characters.

5. Use one or more graphic organizers to prepare a presentation. Some graphic organizers to consider are a Storyboard Organizer, a KWL (Know/Want/Learned) Organizer, a Venn diagram, or a 5Ws and How Web. This type of presentation is designed to appeal to a person's ability to reason or to a person's ability to feel emotions. Arrange your arguments so that they: (1) ask a question and then answer it;
   (2) relate an anecdote, observation, or experience; and
   (3) state a fact or statistic.

6. Use a Book Report organizer such as the Book Report Outline on pages 10 and 31 to plan a report on a biography of a famous person. As you prepare the report, think about your reactions to the events in the historical figure's life that please or bother you, situations that surprise or dazzle you, and obstacles that challenge or disappoint you.

7. Use Venn diagrams such as on pages 26 and 93 to compare and contrast people, places, and socially significant happenings being studied. *Example:* Compare and contrast the differing opinions of opposing political candidates, economic predictions of financial analysis, cases for and against a proposed highway expansion.

8. Construct line graphs, picot graphs, bar graphs, or circle graphs to organize and present data related to class surveys, research findings, or community poll results.

9. Use time lines to establish the chronology of important events such as the sequence of events leading up to a war, the history of a major social movement such as the civil rights or women's suffrage movement or the life of a famous person.

10. Identify cause and effect situations and construct a cause and effect chart to show the sequence and impact. *Example:* Graphically show the influence of technology in today's schools on the workplace of tomorrow.

BIBLIOGRAPHY

of
Related Incentive Publications Products

20-th Century American Heroes
   by Shirley Cook

Basic/Not Boring Grades K-1: Social Studies
   by Imogene Forte and Marjorie Frank

Basic/Not Boring Grades 2-3: Social Studies
   by Imogene Forte and Marjorie Frank

Basic/Not Boring, Grades 4-5: Problem Solving
   by Imogene Forte and Marjorie Frank

*Basic/Not Boring, Grades 4-5: U.S. History,
Government, & Citizenship*
   by Imogene Forte and Marjorie Frank

Booh A Brations!
   by Jan Grubb Philpot

Book-A-Tivities!
   by Jan Grubb Philpot

Celebrate with Books
   by Imogene Forte and Joy MacKenzie

Challenges & Choices
   by Nancy Ullinskey and Lori Hibbert

*Character Education Book of Plays
Elementary Level*
   by Judy Truesdell Mecca

Cooperative Learning Guide & Planning Pak
   by Imogene Forte and Joy MacKenzie

Creating Connections
   by Dorothy Michener

*Curriculum and Project Planner for
Integrating Learning Styles, Thinking Skills,
and Authentic Assessment, Revised Edition*
   by Imogene Forte and Sandra Schurr

Environmental Bulletin Boards
   by Lynn Brisson

*Five-Minute Warm-Ups for Elementary
Grades, Revised Edition*
   by Bea Green, Sandra Schlichting,
   and Mary Ellen Thomas

Graphic Organizers and Planning Outlines
   by Imogene Forte and Sandra Schurr

How to Write a Great Research Paper
   by Leland Graham and Darriel Ledbetter

I've Got Me and I'm Glad
   by Cherrie Farnette, Imogene Forte,
   and Barbara Loss

Including the Special Needs Child
   by Grace Bickert

Inventions & Extensions
   by Doris Spivack and Geri Blond

Internet Adventures
   by Catherine H. Cook
   and Janet M. Pfeifer

*Standards-Based SOCIAL STUDIES
Graphic Organizers & Rubrics for Elementary Students*

Internet Quest
  by Catherine H. Cook
  and Janet M. Pfeifer

Learning Through Research
  by Shirley Cook

Learning to Learn
  by Gloria Frender

Multicultural Plays
  by Judy Truesdell Mecca

One Nation, Fifty States,
  Revised Edition
  by Imogene Forte

People Need Each Other
  by Cherrie Farnette, Imogene Forte,
  and Barbara Loss

Pineapples, Penguins, and Pagodas
  by Barbara Jinkins

Plays That Teach
  by Judy Truesdell Mecca

Risk It!
  by Cathy Griggs Newton

Standards-Based Language Arts
  Graphic Organizers & Rubrics
  for Elementary Students
  by Imogene Forte and Sandra Schurr

Standards-Based Math
  Graphic Organizers & Rubrics
  for Elementary Students
  by Imogene Forte and Sandra Schurr

Standards-Based Science
  Graphic Organizers & Rubrics
  for Elementary Students
  by Imogene Forte and Sandra Schurr

Student Planner and Study Guide
  for Social Studies Success
  by Imogene Forte and Sandra Schurr

Study Skills for Successful Learning
  CD-ROM
  Content by Gloria Frender

The Green Team
  by Dorothy Michener

The Me I'm Learning to Be
  by Imogene Forte

U.S. Social Studies Yellow Pages
  by the Kids' Stuff People

Use the News
  by Joan Groeber

Using Literature to Learn about
  Children Around the World
  by Judith Cochran

Using Literature to Learn about
  the First Americans
  by Judith Cochran

Using Literature to Learn
  America's Story
  by Judith Cochran

Standards-Based SOCIAL STUDIES
Graphic Organizers & Rubrics for Elementary Students

INDEX